Guys

MORAL REVOLUTION

THE NAKED TRUTH ABOUT SEXUAL PURITY

KRIS VALLOTTON

& JASON VALLOTTON

MORAL REVOLUTION

40-Day Journey to Purity

WELCOME TO THE JOURNEY.

It's no mistake that you are holding this journal in your hands. It's a tool created **just for you** by people who are 100% passionate about you stepping into God's amazing best for your body, your sexuality, your relationships, and your life. This forty-day journal will take you on a journey into the deep caverns of God's divine design. You will discover the truth of the way God designed you to function sexually and you will learn the skill of managing your appetite nobly. You will grow in your ability to cultivate healthy, honorable relationships with women, which will ultimately prepare you to find and marry the woman of your dreams.

Kris and Jason Vallotton wrote this journal as a companion to their book Moral Revolution. Each day begins with a quote from the book and then dives deeper into the foundational truths that support the points made in the book. If you want to get the most out of these resources, we recommend that you use the book and journal together.

This journal should take you about **15 minutes** a day to complete, though you can always take more time with it if you want to. And if you really want to get the most out of it, the main thing you need to do is to be brutally honest with yourself. This may be painful at times, but it's the only way that true transformation takes place in our lives.

Each day, you will have the opportunity to practice being honest by answering questions and completing a self-evaluation test. Each self-evaluation consists of six statements that describe the attitudes and behaviors of a person who is pursuing God's standards in their life. Measuring yourself with these statements is not meant to discourage you, but to assist you in **reaching your goals** with God's help!

Finally, each day of this journal quotes a statistic or fact about sexuality and relationships in our society. Hopefully some of these will help you feel that you're not the only one in your situation! Others point to some major problems in our world. We included these not to discourage you, but to describe exactly why the world needs an amazing man like you to rise up, defy the status quo, and do your part to turn the tide in your generation. We believe in you, and more importantly, **God believes in you!**

Let the journey begin!

WHAT'S IT ABOUT?

This journal was created for you by people who are 100% passionate about seeing you experience health and freedom in every area of your life! It will equip you to walk in a greater understanding of how God created you, and His design for sexuality and relationships.

WHAT DO I GET?

- Daily Truths
- Daily Quizzes
- Real and Raw Testimonies
- Character Challenges
- Compelling Stats
- Scriptures
- Reflection and Activation Opportunities
...and so much more!

WHO IS IT FOR?

- Teenagers
- Youth Pastors/Leaders
- Parents
- Small Group Leaders
- Young Adults
- College Pastors
- Married Couples
- Sunday School Teachers

HOW TO USE THE BOOK

 1 Scan the QR Code

 2 Read the Moral Revolution Book Quote

 3 Review the Daily Truth

 4 Read the Testimony

 5 Answer the Interactive Questions

 6 Take the Daily Test...be sure to keep track of your scores!

 7 Respond to the Activation

 8 Engage with God

 9 Fill out the evaluation at the end of each 10-day section

TABLE OF CONTENTS

"Johnny began... a grueling schedule that left him no time for school activities, sports, dances or dating. But he reassured himself that sacrificing for the woman of his dreams would be worth it." (page 25)

DAILY TRUTH
CHARACTER: THE FRUIT OF MANAGING YOUR DESIRE

In many ways, Johnny was just a normal kid with ordinary dreams and simple desires. But what he did with them was radical. Johnny decided to live a purpose-driven life.

Some people think that character is all about saying "no" to things, as if the goal in life is to be able to say, "I've never smoked, never gotten drunk, never had sex, and never done drugs." But imagine someone coming up to Johnny and saying, "Wow, bro, you don't get smashed with your buddies, you don't chase girls, and you don't smoke. You must be a strong person because of all the things you don't do." I imagine Johnny would probably say, "It's not what I don't do that makes me strong, it's what I have chosen to do."

When you define who you are by what you don't do, you partner with a poverty mindset. This way of thinking imprisons you with rules and tries to punish you into purity. But when your standards come from who you are, you live a purpose-driven life, and poverty and powerlessness are defeated on the battlefield of true character.

Character will dictate your boundaries. More specifically, saying "no" to premarital sex only makes sense because you are saying "yes" to being a noble and virtuous guy. ★

I'M NOT A STRONG PERSON BECAUSE OF WHAT I DON'T DO...

Summary: A purpose-driven life makes a complete fool out of sin!

SOUND WISDOM

Take delight in the LORD, and he will give you your heart's desires.

Psalm 37:4 NLT

If you abide in Me and My words abide in you, you will ask what you desire, and it shall be done for you.

John 15:7 NKJV

These two verses reveal that God is not saying "no" to the dreams and desires of your heart. He is the One who put them in you in the first place. And, as their Chief Engineer and Divine Creator, He is the best One to teach you how to manage them.

Whether or not you have a father figure in your life who you can talk to about sex and girls, you can always start by talking to God. Like any good father, He wants you to come to Him with your questions so that together you can work through the challenges of managing your feelings. Best of all, no one believes in you like He does. He is supremely confident in you!

REAL STORY

Most of my life, I have attempted to control, stifle, and sometimes completely disown my desires. Unfortunately, when dealing with sexual desire and longing for intimacy, I was unaware that they could be expressed in a healthy way. More often than not, I would try to fool myself into thinking that I didn't really have those desires, or that they were from the devil and I should try to rebuke them. If I was attracted to a woman or noticed that she had a nice body, instead of being able to simply admit, "She is pretty and there's something I see in her that I'm attracted to," I would deny the feelings of attraction in the guise of "staying pure."

I discovered that we are not powerful enough to deny the desires God has created in us from coming to fruition, and if we go too long with ignoring them, they will come out one way or another. The longer I denied my natural sexual desires, the stronger and more uncontrollable my urges got, and after labeling these desires as bad, the only way for them to surface were through perverse versions of the beautiful desires God had planted in me. Without a healthy way to express my sexuality and longing for intimacy, I turned to placating these desires with masturbation and pornography. Of course, this never came close to touching the desires God had put in me and left me wanting even more than before, with a huge side of guilt and shame.

It wasn't until God dealt with my shame that I was able to fully embrace my desires. Through a series of events, I was able to lay all my shame before the Lord—all of my shortcomings, failures, disappointments…everything. I didn't hide anything from Him. And His response blew me off my feet. I felt Him looking at me with kind eyes. I was so shocked to see such genuine love, and even the sense that He missed me and had been waiting for me. There wasn't any look of disappointment or disgust, which I had thought I would surely find. He showed me that no matter how big a hole I dug or how bad I messed things up, His love is greater and He will always be there eagerly awaiting my return.

With the shame gone, I was able to talk with God about my desires. When I saw a woman I was physically attracted to, I was able to admit it and talk to God about it. It was revolutionary for my life. Instead of hiding some of the deepest longings of my heart from God, I was able to invite Him in and He began teaching me! He showed me how He had handcrafted my heart and placed every hope and longing I've ever felt inside it. He told me that the pain and emptiness I had been feeling was meant to be there, because He would not let any of His children continue on in life missing the gifts He had prepared for them. He wouldn't take away the pain, because the pain was an indicator that there actually was something missing that only He could help me find.

The biggest revelation that has changed my life is realizing that I can trust God with taking care of my heart. He is completely aware of my wants and needs (He is their author) and understands how to meet them more then I could ever hope to. Now as a single person I still experience sexual urges and even sexual frustration from time to time, but instead of hiding from the urges, I tell God, "Thank you that the desires of my heart are alive and well. I know that You made them to be 100% met. And I'm okay with waiting and being frustrated because I know where You take me will meet those needs 10 times better than anything I can do on my own. So, Father, I completely trust You. Continue to teach me about what you have put inside of me."

Brenden
AGE 25 CALIFORNIA, USA

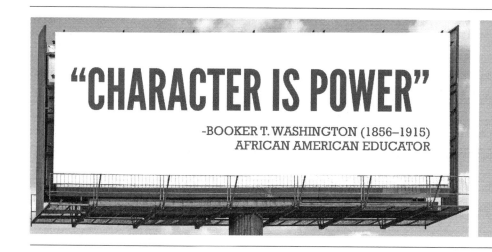

> ## "CHARACTER IS POWER"
> –BOOKER T. WASHINGTON (1856–1915)
> AFRICAN AMERICAN EDUCATOR

Psychologists say that 95–97% of the people in the world do NOT have written goals and fail. While 3–5% have written goals and succeed.

Source: www.busywomenfitness.com

INTERACT

Do you believe God designed your desire for sex and intimate relationship?

Do you believe that He says "yes" to this desire?

Do you believe that He wants to teach you and help you as you manage this desire?

Write down 3 rules you have learned about sex from your parents, peers or teachers:

1)

2)

3)

How many of these are "no" or "don't" rules?

What are you saying "yes" to that explains the need for you to say no to these things?
(If you don't know, don't worry. That's why you are going through this journal!)

CHARACTER
TEST

	STRONGLY DISAGREE	MOSTLY DISAGREE	AGREE SOMEWHAT	MOSTLY AGREE	STRONGLY AGREE
I want to understand both what I am saying "yes" to and what I am saying "no" to when I make a choice, and I want my choices to be consistent with my values and goals.	1	2	3	4	5
I often set short-term goals for myself and am pretty good about reaching them.	1	2	3	4	5
If I don't reach a goal I have set, I don't beat myself up. I just try again.	1	2	3	4	5
I know the kind of person I want to be. When I act beneath my identity, I apologize, make it right, and get back on track.	1	2	3	4	5
I have relationships I care about deeply and fight to protect.	1	2	3	4	5
I am fighting to become a man who can pursue and protect the heart of the woman of my dreams.	1	2	3	4	5

Score:

(Note: Add up your scores after every ten days and evaluate your progress.)

ACTIVATION

Set up a reminder system for yourself today. It could be a timer or alarm on your phone, or a good, old-fashioned piece of string tied around your finger. Use the reminder to ask yourself why you are doing whatever you happen to be doing at the moment. Ask, "What am I saying 'yes' to right now, and why? What am I saying 'no' to, and why?" The more you know the reasons for your choices, the more proactive you can be about them.

TALK TO GOD

Have a conversation with God today about the desire He gave you for sex and relationship.

Thank Him for these gifts, and invite Him to teach you how to manage this desire.

"Your virginity is a treasure hidden in the vault of your life, protected by the helmet of your virtues, values and principles." (page 47)

DAILY TRUTH
WHY VIRGINITY IS A TREASURE

We all love superheroes because we all wish we had superpowers. Be honest, what guy wouldn't want to have razorblades shoot out of his hands like Wolverine? Better yet, which of us wouldn't kill to have Batman's setup? That guy's got more gadgets than Best Buy!

I bet you have never thought of your sexuality as a superpower. But think about it…you have the power to create another human being.

When it comes to sex, you need to be thinking more like Batman than the Joker! Make no mistake about it: sex is power. That's why your virginity is so valuable and why there is such an intense battle (both outside and inside you) over how you are going to use your sexuality. And like all superpowers, it can be used for great good, or for great evil. Whether you realize it or not, you are a superhero writing your own story by the way you manage your sexual superpowers. And regardless of how you feel, you are the only one who can decide if you are going to use your power to manipulate and destroy, or to protect and bring life. ★

MAKE NO MISTAKE ABOUT IT: SEX IS POWER!

Summary:
"With great power comes great responsibility."

—Ben Parker to his nephew, Peter Parker (Spiderman)

Or didn't you realize that your body is a sacred place, the place of the Holy Spirit? Don't you see that you can't live however you please, squandering what God paid such a high price for? The physical part of you is not some piece of property belonging to the spiritual part of you. God owns the whole works. So let people see God in and through your body.

1 Corinthians 6:19–20 MSG

Jesus knows how to handle God-given power. He not only used His power to heal people, He used it to manage His body, including His sex drive. (Yes, Jesus had one too!) If you take a look into His story, you will learn not only how to handle yourself, but more importantly, how to thrive in a world that's raging against all virtues! God wants you to wrap your brain around the idea that your body is not your own. It's holy, set apart, and designed to show the world who's your Daddy!

Jesus revealed that your body is actually God's palace. When people walk by your "house" and look in the windows, so to speak, they ought to be able to say, "Wow, God's home." Your body and your sex drive are beautiful and powerful. For His sake and yours, keep it that way.

REAL STORY

I'm in a men's purity group at my church. I didn't start going because I was struggling with a pornography issue that I couldn't control. I went because of the way that I had chosen to "control" my sexuality was to not acknowledge my feelings and shut them down. I went because what I needed was to connect to my heart and my emotions. I have a need to connect and feel, but that can be scary when I don't know how to do that.

The men's purity group is not about getting guys to not look at porn as much as getting guys to connect with their hearts and break out of their isolation. The group has a technique that says: "If you want to look at porn, call someone." I started to learn to connect to my emotions by not isolating myself and, instead, reaching out for an emotionally safe connection. I don't just call anyone; I call someone of the same sex who is walking with me through life and will embrace me, not try to fix me. I can't stand it when someone labels me with my struggles and gets more concerned with trying to fix me than connecting with my heart. Walking in purity always requires me to be vulnerable and it's up to me to make sure that the people I walk through life with are safe and want to know my heart and not my "disorders."

I learned an easy acronym called H.A.L.T., which means Hopeless, Angry, Lonely, Tired. I found that generally when I want to isolate myself and self-medicate, I am usually feeling one of these four ways. This gave me power. Instead of getting trapped and falling victim to my feelings, I can do something about them—I can go connect and explore them with someone else. Living a life where my feelings are my friends and I don't have to be afraid of them is kind of weird, but that's where I am. I really don't care about what Christian circles say about living "the right life" if that means I can't be real. I am holy and clean because of God, not myself. God says I'm clean, and the more I believe and act like the man He says I am, the more I will remove the things in my life that contradict that. I am not trying to fix myself; I am getting to know how incredible I am, and the powerful God-made hearts of those around me.

Andy
AGE 27 COLORADO, USA

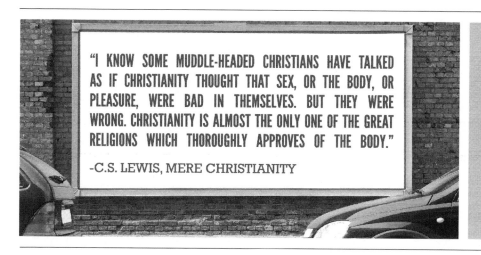

"I KNOW SOME MUDDLE-HEADED CHRISTIANS HAVE TALKED AS IF CHRISTIANITY THOUGHT THAT SEX, OR THE BODY, OR PLEASURE, WERE BAD IN THEMSELVES. BUT THEY WERE WRONG. CHRISTIANITY IS ALMOST THE ONLY ONE OF THE GREAT RELIGIONS WHICH THOROUGHLY APPROVES OF THE BODY."

-C.S. LEWIS, MERE CHRISTIANITY

Most teens (65% of girls and 57% of boys) who have had sex say they wish they had waited.

Source: www.busywomenfitness.com

INTERACT

Have you ever thought of your sexuality as a power to be managed—a power with which you can do either good or evil?

How would you approach your sexuality differently if you thought of it like a superpower?

Have you ever thought of your body as God's house?

Write down 3 things you could change in the way you think about or treat your body in order to truly treat it like His holy home:

1)

2)

3)

BODY ATTITUDE
TEST

	STRONGLY DISAGREE	MOSTLY DISAGREE	AGREE SOMEWHAT	MOSTLY AGREE	STRONGLY AGREE
I love my body. It is a very valuable gift from God.	1	2	3	4	5
My body's capacity for sex is a powerful thing, and I can either use it constructively or destructively.	1	2	3	4	5
There are things I don't do with or to my body because I consider my body holy.	1	2	3	4	5
It is my job to manage my physical appetites, including my sex drive.	1	2	3	4	5
God won't control my sex drive for me, but He will help me learn how to control it.	1	2	3	4	5
I want God to be pleased with the way I take care of our "house."	1	2	3	4	5

Score:

(Note: Add up your scores after every ten days and evaluate your progress.)

ACTIVATION

Pick one thing from the list you wrote that you can do today to treat your body like God's house.

TALK TO GOD

Thank God for your body today. Tell Him everything you like about it. Tell Him what you like about your sexuality.

Ask Him what He thinks about it and how He wants you to treat it.

"For most of us, keeping our purity is not merely a matter of exercising self-control over our sex drives. The world we live in is a minefield just daring us to try and scale the hill of holiness. We are surrounded on all sides by aggressive messages designed to get us to confuse love for lust, and we're surrounded by a bunch of people who have bought into these lies."

(page 51)

DAILY TRUTH
THE BATTLE BETWEEN LOVE AND LUST

There's a true story of a man who died and joined a line of people waiting to pass through the gates of heaven. He overheard each person ahead of him being asked one simple question before they were allowed to enter Paradise: "Did you learn to love?" Some people answered with a joyous, "Yes!" Others had to admit they never learned that lesson very well.

When it was the man's turn to answer the question, he heard God say, "It's not time for you to come in yet. You have to go back and remind the world that this is the question they will have to answer."

If protecting your purity is the battle, then learning to love is the war—the whole purpose of your time on earth. In both cases, victory will be impossible unless you understand what love is. The world stamps the word "love" on all kinds of things—feelings, actions, desires, preferences—which ultimately creates a ton of confusion, especially in the realm of sex and relationships. A good rule to remember is this: Love is giving yourself to benefit another person. Lust cares only about personal gratification while it drains the life out of the world around it.

As Paul the apostle pointed out, it is possible to do a lot of good things that appear totally unselfish and sacrificial, like giving to the poor, and still not have love (see 1 Cor. 13:3)! In the same way, sex and love are easy to confuse because sex is a good thing. When you're "in love" with someone it can feel like sex is the most obvious way you both want to love each other. But it is not always the best thing. Love is a choice, and love always chooses the best. ★

Summary: Love is giving yourself to benefit another person. Lust cares only about personal gratification.

SOUND WISDOM

Love never gives up. Love cares more for others than for self. Love...doesn't force itself on others, Isn't always "me first," Doesn't fly off the handle, Doesn't keep score of the sins of others... [It] puts up with anything... Always looks for the best, Never looks back, But keeps going to the end.

1 Corinthians 13: 4–7 MSG

This is how God loves you. He always looks for the best for you. He cares more for you than He does for Himself. That may sound hard to believe, but it's true. And the first lesson of learning to love is learning to receive His love for you. The more you receive and experience His love for you, the more you will know real love and be able to spot counterfeit love in an instant. The main reason so many people around you (and maybe you too) have bought into all the fakes is that they have never experienced real love in the first place.

A non-negotiable element of any battle plan for purity is to have frequent encounters with God's love. Set aside some time to just hang out with Jesus so that you can encounter Him any way He wants you to.

REAL STORY

One day I was in a church meeting, very much feeling like I was at the end of myself. I knew I needed a touch of God in my life, any kind of touch. During the announcements, I turned my attention to Jesus and immediately felt what I can only describe as something physically pulling my heart out of my chest. As the meeting went on, the feeling didn't subside. Jesus began to speak of His passionate and fierce love for me. In an instant, I understood the meaning of God's jealous love—not a selfish love, but a love that places an immeasurably high value on such an immeasurably small person. I came away from that encounter having experienced the unrelenting, passionate love of Jesus.

But Jesus hadn't finished with me yet. Over the following days and weeks, He started to reveal His love to me as more than just a fiery encounter every now and again, but as a steadfast and enduring, constant reality. He took me back to His life on earth and I saw His love revealed, not just in the cross, but in every second of every day of those 33 years. His final act of dying on the cross is the greatest act of love ever known, but to get there He had to steadfastly choose to love me through every hardship, temptation, and persecution offered by the world. He refused to love Himself more than He loved me, valuing my life far more than His own comforts. And that is love—to value someone so highly that your every action and thought is shaped by what is best for them.

Matt
AGE 23 ENGLAND

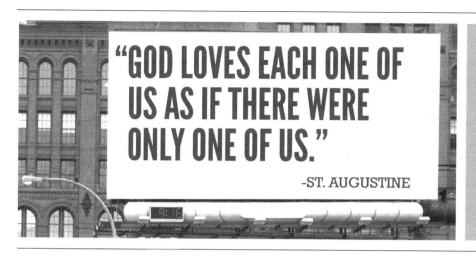

"GOD LOVES EACH ONE OF US AS IF THERE WERE ONLY ONE OF US."

-ST. AUGUSTINE

Teens overwhelmingly value virginity and waiting, regardless of their personal decision. More than 9 in 10 agree that being a virgin is a "good thing."

Source:
"Virginity and the First Time," Henry J. Kaiser Foundation.

INTERACT

Describe one example of what the world calls "love" that doesn't line up with the description of God's love in 1 Corinthians 13.

Write down 3 different ways you have experienced God's love.

1)

2)

3)

LOVE TEST

	STRONGLY DISAGREE	MOSTLY DISAGREE	AGREE SOMEWHAT	MOSTLY AGREE	STRONGLY AGREE
I know God loves me, because I experience it as a reality, not just know about it as an idea or truth in the Bible.	1	2	3	4	5
God knows me and likes me, even though I am not perfect and am still learning to love.	1	2	3	4	5
God is passionate in His pursuit of my heart.	1	2	3	4	5
I trust God's love and know that He will never give up on me.	1	2	3	4	5
God enjoys hanging out with me and wants me to be myself.	1	2	3	4	5
I can talk to God about anything.	1	2	3	4	5

Score:

(Note: Add up your scores after every ten days and evaluate your progress.)

ACTIVATION

Memory Challenge! Copy this verse on a 3x5 card and either take it with you or post it somewhere you'll see it often. Try to memorize it: "The LORD your God is with you, he is mighty to save. He will take great delight in you, he will quiet you with his love, he will rejoice over you with singing." (Zephaniah 3:17 NIV)

TALK TO GOD

Invite the Lord to encounter you with His love today…love that will ROCK YOU!

August 22

Got up late and ran halfway to school...stressed me out. I hate mornings. First day of high school sort of freaked me out...WHATEVER...at least I wasn't the only one stressed out!

Something crazy happened today...I was crossing the road when this ring caught my eye. For whatever reason, I stopped to check it out and everything went mental on me...it was like I saw into the future, but not a pic of me. I saw a vision of some woman. I guess this is what happens when puberty kicks in! ☹

*"Sometimes before you can beat the Goliaths of your life,
you have to take on your brothers (see 1 Sam. 17:1–58)."*
(page 53)

DAILY TRUTH
PEER PRESSURE: TAKING ON YOUR BROTHERS

For most people, being caught between an insecure bully on one side and a bunch of skeptical, jealous, critical friends on the other is the ultimate social nightmare. It's a rare person who can stand up to both and do what needs to be done. David not only did it, he did it with so much style that everyone else in Israel looked lame. How did he do it?

First of all, David never ran with the crowd. He hung out in the fields worshiping God and protecting his father's sheep (a vulnerable and valuable asset, much like your purity) from ravaging wolves, lions and bears. He conquered his insecurity with God in private long before he had a face-off with his insecure peers.

Don't worry, being courageous doesn't mean that you don't have fear. It means that you don't let fear tell you what to do! It also doesn't mean being a loner. Winning the battle for your purity requires the support of a strong community that calls you to a high standard.

But if you want positive peer pressure in your life, it's important to realize that it's created best by people like David who can think for themselves, know who they are in God, and do what is right, whether anyone else is doing it or not. ★

DAVID NEVER RAN WITH THE CROWD...

Summary: David was best friends with the God of the impossible. The insecurity of others couldn't shake his security in God.

SOUND WISDOM

I sought the LORD, and he answered me; he delivered me from all my fears. Those who look to him are radiant; their faces are never covered with shame. (Psalm 34:4–5 NIV)

There is no room in love for fear. Well-formed love banishes fear. Since fear is crippling, a fearful life—fear of death, fear of judgment—is one not yet fully formed in love. (1 John 4:18 MSG)

Most people try to use things like anger, control, and apathy to overcome their fears. But there is only one true antidote to fear—love. Only God's perfect love can free you forever from your insecurities, and the good news is that all you have to do is receive it. David simply "sought the Lord," and the Lord removed all his fears. Wow! Can you imagine what it must feel like to have someone say something that totally wipes out your fear? Well, you don't have to just imagine. If God did it for David, He can and will do it for you.

Casting your cares on the Lord is not a one-time deal; it needs to be a lifestyle—a growing skill of recognizing what and why you're afraid, confessing it to the Lord, and letting His love and truth align your heart with His reality.

REAL STORY

Growing up, I'm pretty certain I was the most insecure person I knew. Even my insecurities seemed to have insecurities! Because of several intense negative experiences with really close friends, I was left feeling alone and worthless. Add those feelings to the jock-style image that high school seems to pound into everyone's head about what a real man looks like. I felt pretty overwhelmed and alone, because I wasn't involved with sports and I wasn't sleeping around like a lot of others were doing. I honestly didn't feel like I met the status quo and was just socially awkward.

I started being real with God about how I was feeling—that I just didn't feel "good enough" and that I even felt disqualified from pursuing future dreams as a result. I kept hearing God telling me these crazy things like, "I absolutely love you! I'm totally for you. I adore who you are as a man...right now!" I decided to try to

trust Him with this. He drove His point home further by giving me the absolute best friends. They all kept reiterating what He was saying. They'd look me in the eye and say, "I fully believe in you. You have what it takes!"

As a result of this constant love and truth from God, and consciously making the choice to not give up hope and to keep believing His truth over my emotions, I now understand who I am so much more and I am able to be confident in who God made me to be: a man who is loved and has what it takes for anything and everything.

Chris
AGE 23 CALIFORNIA, USA

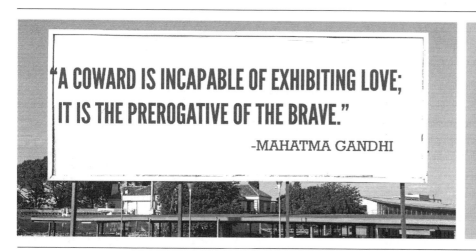

"A COWARD IS INCAPABLE OF EXHIBITING LOVE; IT IS THE PREROGATIVE OF THE BRAVE."

-MAHATMA GANDHI

More than 20% of teens say that "pressure from friends" is a reason they send sexually suggestive messages and images.

Source: http://www.thenationalcampaign.org

INTERACT

We all deal with fear and insecurity. The question is, are you aware of your fears and how are you dealing with them? Write down your three greatest fears or insecurities:

1)

2)

3)

What are three things you do when you feel afraid?:

1)

2)

3)

PEER PRESSURE TEST

	STRONGLY DISAGREE	MOSTLY DISAGREE	AGREE SOMEWHAT	MOSTLY AGREE	STRONGLY AGREE
When I feel stressed, I can usually identify the cause of the stress.	1	2	3	4	5
It's important for me to know how to face and manage my fears so I can be true to myself and to God.	1	2	3	4	5
I make sure that my close friends are people who won't pressure me to do things that conflict with my commitment to God.	1	2	3	4	5
I care about what people think of me, but I care more what God thinks of me.	1	2	3	4	5
I often confess my fears to God.	1	2	3	4	5
I want to be a man of courage who consistently overcomes my fears and does the right thing.	1	2	3	4	5

Score:

(Note: Add up your scores after every ten days and evaluate your progress.)

ACTIVATION

Pick one area of insecurity you struggle with—it could be talking to a girl, speaking your mind, or trying out for a play or the basketball team. Challenge yourself to do one thing, no matter how small, to face your fear and do it anyway.

TALK TO GOD

Follow David's advice and have a conversation with God today about insecurity.
Expect His answer, which can't help but express perfect love, to be exactly what you need to hear.

"…the billion-dollar question is: Who do you think you are? Our behavior flows from the vision that we have for ourselves. Once we decide who we are, then we will naturally work out our actions, attitudes, and behaviors to manifest our person." (page 63)

DAILY TRUTH
VISION: FINDING THE ONE…OR BECOMING THE ONE

It's fun to fantasize about meeting the girl of your dreams. No doubt that magical meeting will inspire all sorts of amazing feelings in you—that you can take on the world, that you want to be a better man, that you will do anything to have her. But don't make the mistake of thinking that you should wait for her to inspire those feelings before you take on the world. Truthfully, it's pretty easy to "get the girl." The real challenge is not finding the woman of your dreams, but becoming the man of her dreams.

Role models are essential to forming a vision for the man you want to become. Lists of good character traits don't mean much until you see them in action. So before you ask, "Who do I want to be?" you should ask, "Who do I want to be like?"

As you look for role models, remember that it can be tough to tell the difference between noble men and cool boys in a culture that defines "success" in terms of money and fame. Most of the "cool" athletes, actors, musicians, and Wall Street "masters of the universe" are just overgrown, insecure boys with the talent to create an image that looks powerful but has nothing to do with true character. You may have to look a bit harder for the real heroes, but they are out there! ★

WHO DO I WANT TO BE LIKE?…

Summary: Find real heroes. Finding them is the first step to becoming one of them.

SOUND WISDOM

Watch what God does, and then you do it, like children who learn proper behavior from their parents. Mostly what God does is love you. Keep company with Him and learn a life of love. Observe how Christ loved us. His love was not cautious but extravagant. He didn't love in order to get something from us but to give everything of himself to us. Love like that.

Ephesians 5:1–2 MSG

The world is desperate for men who love like Christ—extravagantly, not cautiously. Love is completely opposed to all forms of fear. Jesus modeled a fearless life. He bravely walked on raging seas, calmly rebuked demons, ferociously kicked the Pharisees' butts, generously fed thousands, and then went to hell itself to wipe out the devil. Jesus was a man's man. How was He able to do all of that? Jesus knew who He was and whose He was!

He takes great pleasure in helping you flourish, and if you let Him, He will lead you into joy—the joy of being a man who brings strength to those around him, a man whose heart is free and alive with extravagant love. In order to do this, you need to see yourself the way God sees you. Once you can do that, your identity is sealed in Him.

REAL STORY

Being raised in a broken home, I lacked a role model through my childhood and most of my teenage years. Fortunately, after I started following Jesus at sixteen, I was surrounded by awesome men who inspired greatness in me. One of them was my pastor for two years. Although I didn't have a very close personal relationship with him, there was something about him that made me want to be a better man. However, the man who has shaped me the most is the man I have served for the past two years. He is both an amazing leader and an amazing father. He has shown me how to do "ministry" well, but more than that, he has shown me how to do life well.

One of the things I have learned from him is to truly believe in people. He sees people according to their potential, not according to their shortcomings. In fact, he believes in people before they believe in themselves. Those who spend even a short amount of time with him leave feeling extremely encouraged. He is very intentional about speaking life over people on a daily basis. I now find myself calling out the gold in others as he did for me.

This man has taught me how to live life with a strong sense of purpose. He is known for being extremely intentional about everything that he does. He is purposeful about how he spends his time and who he spends it with. He lives in a way that tells you that he has an assignment. At the same time, those who are touched by him never feel like they are a project. This is because he has learned to keep the main thing the main thing—loving God and loving people. I hope that I have learned the same thing. And for him I am very thankful.

Chuck
AGE 34 CANADA

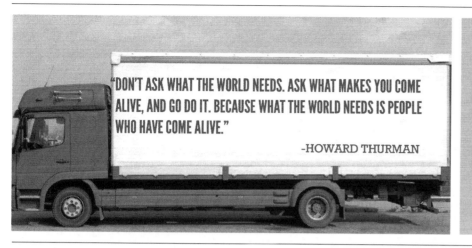

"DON'T ASK WHAT THE WORLD NEEDS. ASK WHAT MAKES YOU COME ALIVE, AND GO DO IT. BECAUSE WHAT THE WORLD NEEDS IS PEOPLE WHO HAVE COME ALIVE."

—HOWARD THURMAN

According to a survey of adults aged 20 to 59, women have an average of four sex partners during their lifetime; men have an average of seven.

Source: http://www.cdc.gov

INTERACT

Describe three men—real or fictional—who are true heroes and lovers like Jesus:

1)

2)

3)

How can you follow the example set by these men?

VISION
TEST

	STRONGLY DISAGREE	MOSTLY DISAGREE	AGREE SOMEWHAT	MOSTLY AGREE	STRONGLY AGREE
I want to be a man who lives for something greater than myself.	1	2	3	4	5
I want to be a man who loves people extravagantly like Jesus does.	1	2	3	4	5
I want to become the man deserved by the woman of my dreams.	1	2	3	4	5
I want to be a man who can take responsibility and commit to things.	1	2	3	4	5
I want to be a man who can fight for a worthy cause.	1	2	3	4	5
I want to be a man who can love a good woman fully, without withholding myself from her.	1	2	3	4	5

Score:
(Note: Add up your scores after every ten days and evaluate your progress.)

ACTIVATION

Media Challenge! What media/entertainment is influencing your personal vision, and what fruit is it producing in your life? Take a break from your daily dose of video games, sports, action movies, and magazines and challenge yourself to grow your personhood. Take the time you would normally be using to entertain yourself and use it to build yourself up. Dust off your Bible and find as many scriptures as you can about how you were made and who you are. Once you have done that, spend time making them real to you by thinking and praying about them. Here's one to start with: Jeremiah 1:5.

TALK TO GOD

Ask God to reveal His vision for your character and success.

Ask Him what it means to become "the one" for the woman of your dreams.

"Virtues help us to live from the inside out instead of from the outside in. No longer do I live by other people's rules. Instead, I live by values that guide my attitudes, which, in turn, determine my choices. Choices dictate my behavior. My behaviors become manifestations of my personhood, and my personhood leads me into my destiny." (page 66)

DAILY TRUTH
VIRTUES, PART 1: LAYING OUT YOUR BOUNDARIES

Jesus lived from the inside out. He said, "…I freely lay down my life. And so I am free to take it up again. No one takes it from me. I lay it down of my own free will" (John 10:17–18 MSG). He was in full command of His choices. Life was not happening to Him; He was happening to life!

Jesus often pointed out that His choices were fully aligned with whatever His Father was doing and saying. This central relationship with His Dad defined the boundaries of His choices from day to day, moment to moment. Though constantly confronted by many things—the needs of people, pressure from His disciples, opposition from the enemy and religious leaders, and even His own needs and desires—that could have led Him to act apart from relationship with His Father, He never gave in to them. He was able to say "no" to everything that His Father was not asking Him to do, even things that looked good, holy, and important.

Jesus set the example for you. Your primary responsibility is to align your virtues with His and walk in close relationship and partnership with Him, doing and saying what He is doing and saying. The beautiful thing is that the boundaries of your relationship with Him will make you free and powerful. He is a free and powerful God, and when you join Him in what He is doing, you can't help but become free and powerful like Him. ★

JESUS SET THE EXAMPLE FOR YOU...

Summary: Align your virtues with what Jesus is doing and saying, and you will receive His power to live within the boundaries created by those virtues.

The center of any plan to align your virtues, choices, and boundaries with Jesus must be spending regular, frequent time with Him. These encounters and conversations build your connection with God, which is the true source of your power to live within His boundaries for your life. God doesn't want your boundaries to be motivated by fear of breaking the rules, but by your desire to protect and deepen your heart-to-heart connection with Him.

As you set boundaries to prioritize your relationship with God, remember that they will be tested. And you need this testing in order to grow strong and skillful in keeping those boundaries. Always remember in every test that Jesus has been there before you, knows exactly what you're going through, and has strength, encouragement, and comfort to offer you. He invites you to come boldly to Him and ask for help in any and every situation.

REAL STORY

I grew up with a skewed idea of boundaries. I learned that saying "no" to a request for help was bad. It was taught by my family and the general culture around me that, "If you say 'no' you are 'selfish'" and "You should always put everybody else's needs before your own." I didn't have much of a concept of putting my need for rest before another's need for help. Those things, coupled with not knowing my value, made saying "no" to someone pretty much the most difficult thing ever. Relationships became stressed. I would end up resenting a person asking me for something and resenting myself for not saying "no."

As I began to discover how valuable I really was and learned to make myself a priority, I was freed to say "no." This began an upward cycle of self worth where I said "no" because I valued myself. Every time I said "no," I acknowledged how valuable I was, which improved my self worth even more. This also helped keep my relationships from deteriorating; in fact it actually improved them. I stopped resenting people because I could say "no," which in turn presented people with an opportunity to express their love for me by respecting my boundaries.

Ben
AGE 23 CALIFORNIA, USA

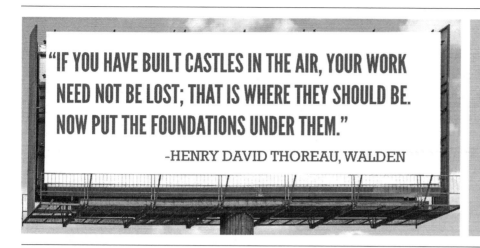

"IF YOU HAVE BUILT CASTLES IN THE AIR, YOUR WORK NEED NOT BE LOST; THAT IS WHERE THEY SHOULD BE. NOW PUT THE FOUNDATIONS UNDER THEM."

-HENRY DAVID THOREAU, WALDEN

1 in 2 teens who have been in a serious relationship say they've gone against their beliefs in order to please their partner.

Source: http://loveisnotabuse.com

INTERACT

Read these words of Jesus that specifically address boundaries for sex.
Then write one or two sentences expressing personal virtues that are based on His words:

1. "But I tell you that anyone who looks at a woman lustfully has already committed adultery with her in his heart" (Matthew 5:28 NIV).

2. "But I tell you that anyone who divorces his wife, except for marital unfaithfulness, causes her to become an adulteress, and anyone who marries the divorced woman commits adultery" (Matthew 5:32 NIV).

3. "Haven't you read in your Bible that the Creator originally made man and woman for each other, male and female? And because of this, a man leaves father and mother and is firmly bonded to his wife, becoming one flesh—no longer two bodies but one. Because God created this organic union of the two sexes, no one should desecrate his art by cutting them apart" (Matthew 19:4–6 MSG).

VIRTUES TEST

	STRONGLY DISAGREE	MOSTLY DISAGREE	AGREE SOMEWHAT	MOSTLY AGREE	STRONGLY AGREE
Living out of virtues should not be rules-driven, but relationship-driven.	1	2	3	4	5
I set boundaries to protect my relationships, especially my relationship with God.	1	2	3	4	5
I want to live from the inside out and take responsibility for all my choices.	1	2	3	4	5
I want to be a person who refuses to give up my virtues, even when I fall short of them.	1	2	3	4	5
I want my values and priorities to line up with the values and priorities of Jesus.	1	2	3	4	5
I am committed to knowing Christ and learning to live like Him as we walk in relationship together.	1	2	3	4	5

Score:

(Note: Add up your scores after every ten days and evaluate your progress.)

ACTIVATION

Spend some time reading the Sermon on the Mount (Matthew 5–7) and write out three more personal virtues based on the words of Christ.

TALK TO GOD

Talk to Jesus about the standard He set for you in His words and actions.

Ask Him to lead you and help you in pursuing that standard.

Ask Him for His wisdom in how to apply His words to the circumstances of your life.

Ask Him for the courage to get back up if you stumble.

Ask Him to lead you into a lifestyle completely defined by your trust in His words and by your friendship with Him.

"Free people can handle liberty because they have developed character through exercising the restraint dictated by their virtues. They are not the slaves of their physical desires; rather, they train their bodies to behave in order to fulfill the higher desires created by their own virtues."

(page 64)

DAILY TRUTH
VIRTUES, PART 2: LIVING IN FREEDOM

God gave you a sex drive, and it's your job to manage it. Underlying this message is a key truth: God wants you—not your parents or your friends or even Himself—to manage your sex drive (and your whole life) because He wants you to be free. God could have programmed us to serve Him, but He couldn't force us to love Him. The very nature of love is that it requires us to be free to choose. Otherwise our relationship with God (and people) would resemble a shotgun wedding, where a couple is forced to marry.

Love requires freedom and freedom is the power to manage yourself! That is why masters of piano, martial ares or sports make what the do seem so effortless— so free. Through constant and ever-refining practice they have developed the strength and the skill to control their bodies.

Becoming masterful in any advanced skill— particularly the skill of managing your appetites (including your sex drive)—is a learning journey. You will have good days and hard days, days of victory and breakthrough, and days of just getting up and doing what you need to do to stay "in shape." You will need the support of the Holy Spirit to coach you as well as people you can trust, like spiritual fathers, mothers, youth pastors and friends. But the most important thing you need to remember is to never quit and keep your eye on love's prize! ★

FREEDOM IS THE POWER TO MANAGE YOURSELF...

Summary: The goal of living in the boundaries set by Christ's words and example is to develop increasing levels of freedom—freedom to love.

SOUND WISDOM

It is absolutely clear that God has called you to a free life. Just make sure that you don't use this freedom as an excuse to do whatever you want to do and destroy your freedom. Rather, use your freedom to serve one another in love. For everything we know about God's Word is summed up in a single sentence: Love others as you love yourself. That's an act of true freedom. Galations 5:13–14 MSG

Your relational boundaries should be driven by God's command to love others as you love yourself. Because freedom is the core of love, this means honoring your own freedom and the freedom of others. It means refusing to let others control you and refusing to control others. Doing this can be tough in a society filled with a lot of people who refuse to control themselves. But no matter what anyone else does, you always have the power and responsibility to choose your response.

The main thing to remember as you learn to walk in increasing levels of freedom is that love is the whole purpose for freedom. As soon as you start using your freedom without love, you'll end up in slavery. Obviously, this means that freedom is not rebellion.

REAL STORY

As the summer of 2011 drew to a balmy close, I embarked from England on a new season of adventure in California. However, this time around it promised to be quite different. The destination was familiar, and the decision for the road ahead was "go!" But understanding the purpose of the next 9 months was another matter entirely.

Life quickly presented itself with little in the way of external controls or imposed structure. There were no real commitments competing for a piece of me. I was afforded the unique opportunity of choosing exactly how to spend my time, all of the time. I discovered something important about myself: I wasn't very good at choosing. And this was my privilege, to discover what really happens when I am in complete control of my time, my life, my spiritual walk, my relationships, my purity, my diet, my fitness, my work, my education, my whatever. Life was neither automatic nor environmental; everything was a choice. This external freedom created a kind of "heart check-up": "How do I live when I have complete freedom?"

With so much freedom, why was I not living the way I wanted? As it turns out, freedom isn't in my circumstances; it comes from within. An environment of external freedom revealed the truth about my internal freedom. With no one telling me what to do, the question became, "What would you do if you could do anything you want?" Someone once said, "You play the hand you're dealt. I think the game's worthwhile." But in my life it has seemed as though the deck of cards were spread across the table, and I, more than ever, was free to pick the cards. So, why not pick a winning hand? As the months rolled on, I discovered increasing levels of internal freedom through my walk with God and my friends. I also picked up many responsibilities along the way.. My freedom has become a weapon of intentionality that I use to live life on purpose through my choices. As I continue to walk this journey with Jesus, my decisions protect my priorities and my days are richer because of it.

Will
AGE 24 ENGLAND

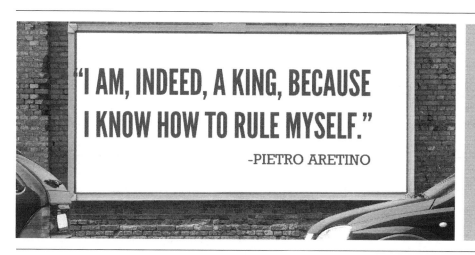

"I AM, INDEED, A KING, BECAUSE I KNOW HOW TO RULE MYSELF."

-PIETRO ARETINO

Nearly 1 in 4 girls who have been in a relationship (23%) reported going further sexually than they wanted as a result of pressure.

Source: http://loveisnotabuse.com

INTERACT

Give an example of how using your freedom in a non-loving way ends up destroying your freedom.

Why is choosing to love others as you love yourself an act of true freedom?

Would you say that freedom—controlling yourselves and not controlling one another—is a shared value in your closest relationships? Why or why not?

FREEDOM TEST

	STRONGLY DISAGREE	MOSTLY DISAGREE	AGREE SOMEWHAT	MOSTLY AGREE	STRONGLY AGREE
Managing my choices within the boundaries created by my virtues is necessary for me to grow in freedom.	1	2	3	4	5
God wants me to be completely free so I can love Him, myself, and others like He does.	1	2	3	4	5
Withholding love will undermine my freedom.	1	2	3	4	5
No matter what anyone else does to me, I am still free to choose whether or not my response will be loving.	1	2	3	4	5
Like football and playing the piano, loving others is a set of skills that I must grow in through consistent, focused practice.	1	2	3	4	5
It is not my job to control the choices of people around me.	1	2	3	4	5

Score:

(Note: Add up your scores after every ten days and evaluate your progress.)

ACTIVATION

Choose three things you can do today to exercise freedom: one thing to show your love for God, one thing to show your love for others, and one thing to show love to yourself.

TALK TO GOD

Ask God to show you how much He cares about freedom and to help you understand His purposes for giving us free will.

Ask Jesus to show you how He always used His freedom to love, and to lead you into that freedom in your own life and relationships.

THIS IS THE ONE!!

AUGUST 23

Officially the worst day EVER! Sooo, after staying up most of the night thinking about that ring, I decided to check it out today... Lets just say I think I'm loosing it! For real's... One second I was looking at the ring and all of the sudden I wound up grabbing this old Sales dude by the arms...What the heck am I doing? Unbelievable...UnfreakinBeliEvAble... I wanted to die! The worst part of itall is that it's not my fault...seriously...it's like a magic Genie jumped out of the diamond ring and talked to me! That chick makes me CRAzy! I can't tell anybody about the ring deal because they'll put m a padded room with 3 square meals a day...

"Guys need to make sure their intimacy level matches their commitment level." (page 74)

DAILY TRUTH
WHO DO YOU WANT TO ATTRACT?

In our day and age, insecurity has become a serial killer! Insecurity has many masks, but left alone it will lead you to violate yourself and the world around you, destroying who you were created to be with high doses of anxiety. Insecurity is often heightened in a relationship for a guy because of these age-old questions: "Do I have what it takes? Do I have what it takes to win her heart? Do I have what it takes to provide? Do I have what it takes to be a man?"

God is the ultimate antidote for insecurity because He always believes in you! But whenever you let a woman (or anyone else) determine whether you have the stuff, you have tethered yourself to the shifting winds of human opinion and left yourself wide open to insecurity. It's not long before you tell your girlfriend that you love her when you don't, or kiss her when you're not committed to her, all because you are fighting to feel secure. As the pain intensifies, so do your actions, and soon you are in bed with someone you have no intention of spending your life with. All you really need to do to avoid this downward spiral is to connect to the correct source of security…God!

In order for your intimacy level to match your level of commitment, you have to be a powerful person. When Jesus is your source, insecurity, fear and whatever is not from Him will be forced to leave. It is from this place of power and protection that you will be able to do what you say you are going to do. And when you can keep your word, you know you are ready to start your pursuit! ★

GOD IS THE ANTIDOTE FOR INSECURITY...

Summary: Pursuing the heart of a good woman begins with becoming a powerful person, and being powerful begins by being humble.

SOUND WISDOM

But he said to me, "My grace is sufficient for you, for my power is made perfect in weakness." Therefore I will boast all the more gladly about my weaknesses, so that Christ's power may rest on me…For when I am weak, then I am strong.

2 Corinthians 12:9–10 NIV

Jesus' intimacy level matched His commitment level. First, He blew up the "real men don't cry" paradigm by being strong enough to be vulnerable. He cried in public. He asked His friends to be there with Him when He faced the darkest night of His life. He loved and trusted men He knew would betray Him. He forgave those who, in ignorance and hatred, destroyed the best thing that had ever happened to them. He was strong enough to feel the full range of human emotion, strong enough to be known, strong enough to risk heartbreak, strong enough to offer love to others without conditions.

Jesus had no problem with intimacy or vulnerability, because God was His ultimate Source for identity and security. When you go to God like Jesus did, He will not only give you His strength; He will show you how to love the way that He loves.

REAL STORY

Growing up, I was extremely shy. At least, that's what I was continuously told by everyone around me. I always assumed there was something wrong with me because this "shyness" seemed to always have a negative connotation. I hated not being like "everybody else," and wondered why I wasn't. Over time, this developed into an intense and overwhelming insecurity that ended up following me into my adult life. I began to use my sexuality, and the fact that girls seemed to be attracted to me, to start meeting my needs. It was the only thing that made me feel good about myself. Even though my original "shyness" had faded somewhat, being around girls, flirting, and making out made me feel so much better. But it was so momentary. At the end of the day, I would still go home feeling alone and depressed.

In looking back, I realize that I was attracting certain girls because of the way I carried myself and treated myself. I was so unsure of who I was, and they were in the exact same position of not feeling known, loved, or valuable. In every one of these situations, we were both looking to each other for purely selfish reasons. We were choosing to meet our needs in an unhealthy, and very temporary, way.

In the last three years of my life, God has taken me on this incredible journey of discovering the real me and I have learned what it looks like to see myself through His eyes. My closest friends have also, time and time again, been there to remind me that I am a son of God, that I have what it takes, and that they truly do believe in me. Learning to love myself and becoming confident in who I am as a man has completely transformed the way I live my life and also the qualities I look for in a woman. It has also very much changed the kind of woman I attract. Confident women are not attracted to insecure men.

Ash
AGE 24 ENGLAND

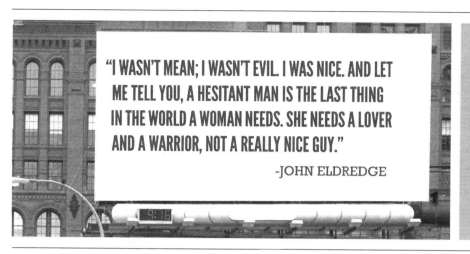

"I WASN'T MEAN; I WASN'T EVIL. I WAS NICE. AND LET ME TELL YOU, A HESITANT MAN IS THE LAST THING IN THE WORLD A WOMAN NEEDS. SHE NEEDS A LOVER AND A WARRIOR, NOT A REALLY NICE GUY."

-JOHN ELDREDGE

Studies show that happiness is contagious and that potential dates find it hard to walk away from happy people. One of the biggest turn-offs during a date is negativity.

Source: Spindel, Janis. How to Date Men: Dating Secrets from America's Top Matchmaker.

INTERACT

What makes you feel powerful as a man? Where do you draw your strength from?

What are some of your main areas of weakness? Do you share these areas with God and with trusted friends?

How comfortable are you receiving strength and help from those who are stronger than you are?

STRENGTH TEST

	STRONGLY DISAGREE	MOSTLY DISAGREE	AGREE SOMEWHAT	MOSTLY AGREE	STRONGLY AGREE
Being vulnerable about my areas of weakness is actually a strength.	1	2	3	4	5
Jesus wants to bring His strength to my life, and I need it.	1	2	3	4	5
Accepting help from God and others is not a weakness.	1	2	3	4	5
I want to be a man who can bring strength to a woman, not a man who uses a woman to feel strong.	1	2	3	4	5
I want to be a man who can protect a woman who is strong enough to be vulnerable with me.	1	2	3	4	5
I know my areas of weakness and I am working on letting Jesus perfect His strength in those areas.	1	2	3	4	5

Score:

(Note: Add up your scores after every ten days and evaluate your progress.)

ACTIVATION

Can you recognize the difference between false power and real power? Think of a person you are impressed with, a person you would call "powerful," and list some examples of how they express their power. Then compare those examples to Jesus. How are they similar, and how are they different?

TALK TO GOD

David prayed, "Search me, O God, and know my heart…" (Ps. 139:23). It's common to make the mistake of trying to dig through your life and find all your weaknesses and shortcomings. It's better to let God do the digging. Invite Him to search your heart and talk with you about any areas where He wants to bring strength to you.

"It is really impossible to control your behavior long-term unless you master your thoughts and subject them to the virtues that you have chosen to live by." (page 82–83)

DAILY TRUTH
PURITY PLAN, PART 1: TEACHING YOUR SEX DRIVE TO THINK

A divided mind creates confusion and inconsistent behavior and siphons off your power. In contrast, a pure mind is a powerful mind. It has strength because it does not tolerate thoughts that violate your foundation.

Jesus said that His words were "foundational words, words to build a life on" (Mat 7:24 MSG). In the same talk, He clearly said that entertaining lust in your heart is the same as having sex outside marriage. If you intend to have a pure mind then you will need to build an arsenal around the way you think! Remember, any thought that violates love will compromise your foundation and bring destruction into your life.

Building a strong thought life in preparation for marriage is like training for a pro sport. Competitive athletes have extraordinary discipline when training their bodies because they constantly fix their sights on where they are headed. The "big game" puts every distraction in perspective. To maintain this unbroken focus, winners feed their brains on a steady diet of stats, strategies, and past game stories. And they hang out with other athletes and coaches who are all doing the same. They fill their minds with what they need to do to get where they're going, so there is no room for anything else. ★

A PURE MIND IS A POWERFUL MIND...

Summary: When an "out of bounds" thought pops into your brain, you can't just "not think about it." Train yourself to think about something else.

SOUND WISDOM

Keep your eyes on Jesus, who both began and finished this race we're in. Study how he did it. Because he never lost sight of where he was headed…he could put up with anything along the way: Cross, shame, whatever… When you find yourselves flagging in your faith, go over that story again, item by item, that long litany of hostility he plowed through. That will shoot adrenaline into your souls!

Hebrews 12:2–3 MSG

Like a pro athlete, Jesus' focus and attention was constantly filled with the "joy" He had set before Him at the end of His big race—first reconciling you to the Father, and then making you fit for…a wedding. Jesus' entire focus is on preparing Himself and you for a heavenly, eternal marriage, and He tolerates no distractions. It's not too early to set your sights on marriage like Jesus did. The best defense against out-of-bounds thoughts and urges is a mind fully occupied with what your heart really desires—first Jesus, and then your wife.

Paul said to take your thoughts and make them submit to the knowledge of Christ. Practically, this means getting in the habit of asking yourself, "Would Christ be thinking about this woman this way or myself this way?" If you don't know the answer to the question, then ask Him. He is the best "thought trainer" around.

REAL STORY

As a teenager I really had a struggle with feeling condemned over my thought life. Whenever an impure thought came into my head, I felt like I was impure and dirty myself. I gave power to that lie by believing it, and my thought life spiraled out of control. I talked with youth pastors and friends and got prayer for it on numerous occasions, but I always seemed to get back to the same place of feeling dirty and impure.

The biggest thing that helped me get through these times of feeling condemned was having someone tell me that these thoughts were not necessarily mine, but were being suggested by the enemy. When an impure thought came into my mind, instead of trying to not think about it (which is impossible—for example if I tell you not to think about a banana, what's the first thing that comes into your head?), I would choose to think about how God sees me in regards to purity. For example, I would think about truths like "God sees me as pure," "I am a man of purity," "God is going to bring breakthrough to others through my victory in purity." In thinking this way, you immediately shift your focus away from the impure thought and toward the purity that God has for you.

For me, this way of thinking drastically reduced the onset of the random impure thoughts. Maybe, whoever those thoughts were coming from didn't like me meditating on purity, and gave up trying to get me to play their game. Because of this, I was able to give my wife the gift of my virginity. Two years into marriage, my wife and I have an amazing pure sex life and the truth to keep it that way.

Doug
AGE 28 NEW ZEALAND

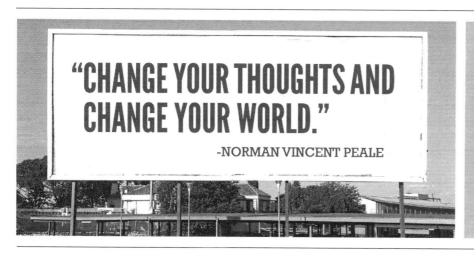

"CHANGE YOUR THOUGHTS AND CHANGE YOUR WORLD."

-NORMAN VINCENT PEALE

Among women aged 15 to 44, average age at first sexual intercourse was 17.3 years. Their male counterparts lost their virginity at 17.0 years on average.

Source: http://www.newstrategist.com

INTERACT

How would your thoughts about girls and sex change if you saw every girl as somebody's daughter or somebody's wife?

Would you want your friends to think about your wife in the way you think about girls? Why or why not?

When you think about girls, do you think only about their bodies, or about their whole beings? What is the significance of this?

What is the difference between wanting a woman and wanting a wife?

Do you think of yourself as a future husband? What does that mean to you?

THOUGHT TEST

	STRONGLY DISAGREE	MOSTLY DISAGREE	AGREE SOMEWHAT	MOSTLY AGREE	STRONGLY AGREE
I am responsible to manage my thoughts and I choose what I will feed my mind.	1	2	3	4	5
I want to think about women the way Jesus does.	1	2	3	4	5
I want to get married, and I am training my thoughts to align with this desire.	1	2	3	4	5
I do not tolerate lustful thoughts about women.	1	2	3	4	5
I think about and look forward to marriage on a regular basis.	1	2	3	4	5
I am training my mind to think of and respect every woman as a whole person and as someone's daughter or potential wife.	1	2	3	4	5

Score:

(Note: Add up your scores after every ten days and evaluate your progress.)

ACTIVATION

Make a list of the top 10 qualities you desire in a wife:

TALK TO GOD

Go over your list with God and ask His opinion on the qualities you wrote down.

Ask Him to help you train your mind and your life to pursue and wait for the marriage He has for you.

"If you are not compromising your heart by what you look at, you will bring wholeness, purity and light into your body. But if your eyes compromise your heart, it will bring darkness into your life." (page 86)

DAILY TRUTH
PURITY PLAN, PART 2: TEACHING YOUR SEX DRIVE TO SEE

Mother Teresa dedicated her life to caring for the poorest of the poor in Calcutta, India. Many people could not fathom why, day in and day out, she touched the lepers and held the dying, fed the orphans and loved those that society had deemed outcast and untouchable. Her reason? "Each one of them is Jesus in disguise," she said. She got this idea from Jesus Himself, who told us that however we treat "the least of these" is actually how we are treating Him (see Mat. 25:40). Mother Teresa believed Jesus' words and trained herself to see every person, even a leper or a starving orphan dying of AIDS, according to their eternal value in Jesus' eyes.

Jesus set the standard for how He wants you to see all women: even those who don't know Him, don't know their value, and don't know who they are. Jesus looked at women with eyes of pure love, and as a result, women like the Samaritan woman at the well, the woman caught in adultery, and many other ladies who had been branded by sexual sin all felt safe with Him. They knew He would neither condemn them nor use them.

EACH ONE OF THEM IS JESUS IN DISGUISE...

Until you train your eyes to see women as daughters of the King, it's easy to see them as sexual objects. Many girls today act like their value is defined by sex, because that is how they have been treated. But it is your job to change that. ★

Summary: Jesus wants you to see women through His eyes, for then you will be able to love as He loves.

SOUND WISDOM

So we fix our eyes not on what is seen, but on what is unseen. For what is seen is temporary, but what is unseen is eternal.

2 Corinthians 4:18 NIV

The things that last the longest are the most real, and the most real things are usually invisible to our naked eyes. So if you want to see what's most real about people, you're going to have to learn to see the invisible. This is how God sees. When Samuel went to search for Israel's new king, he didn't pick David first. He saw Jesse's tall, handsome son, Eliab, and thought he was obviously God's choice. But God said, "Looks aren't everything. Don't be impressed with his looks and stature…God judges differently than humans do. Men and women look at the face; God looks into the heart" (1 Sam. 16:7 MSG). God had chosen a man after His own heart.

God wants to give you His ability to see heart-to-heart. All you have to do is ask Him how He sees people, and soon you will see them like that.

REAL STORY

When I was younger, it seemed like the popular thing to do was to disrespect and demean women, making them little more than sex objects. Hey, all the guys on TV were doing it, right? Growing up in that environment, it isn't surprising that my sex drive at times was like an untamable beast rampaging through a delicate little flower shop. There were times when the urge to look at pornography or fantasize about women seemed insurmountable.

But Jesus gave me a new heart and a new mind. God showed me how pure and beautiful women are created to be. He showed me my role to protect and honor them and cherish them the way Jesus cherishes the church. He showed me how to value women as priceless jewels, and how to war tirelessly in the pursuit of purity.

Now, I see women as the queens, princesses, and daughters that they are.

Now, I see women as sisters and friends, not slaves and objects.

Now, I love serving and protecting women instead of shaming and dishonoring them.

Now, I see the truth. And the Truth has set me free.

Llyod
AGE 25 FLORIDA, USA

"YOU CAN'T DEPEND ON YOUR EYES WHEN YOUR IMAGINATION IS OUT OF FOCUS."

-MARK TWAIN

Among teens surveyed who had not had sex, over three-fourths agreed that they were waiting to have sex when they are in a committed relationship or married.

Source: "Virginity and the First Time," Henry J. Kaiser Foundation.

INTERACT

Have you ever had someone really "see" you on a heart level?

What did that person do or say to make you feel "seen"?

How does seeing someone's heart change your view of them, either positively or negatively?

Have you ever asked Jesus to show you how He sees a certain person?

How did this change your view of that person?

EYE TEST

	STRONGLY DISAGREE	MOSTLY DISAGREE	AGREE SOMEWHAT	MOSTLY AGREE	STRONGLY AGREE
I refuse to see women as sex objects, even if they see themselves that way.	1	2	3	4	5
I want to see and treat people as "Jesus in disguise."	1	2	3	4	5
I want to be able to see past the physical and see from God's eternal perspective into people's hearts.	1	2	3	4	5
I am training myself not to judge or value people according to their physical appearance.	1	2	3	4	5
I want to see women as Jesus sees them.	1	2	3	4	5
I want to be seen for who I really am.	1	2	3	4	5

Score:

(Note: Add up your scores after every ten days and evaluate your progress.)

ACTIVATION

Think of someone in your life who is "poor"—someone who needs a kind word, a friend, some money or food, or just a hug. What is one thing you could do to treat that person as "Jesus in disguise"? Go for it!

TALK TO GOD

In his letter to the Ephesian church, Paul said, "I pray also that the eyes of your heart may be enlightened…" (Eph. 1:18 NIV).

Ask God to enlighten the eyes of your heart to see those around you as Jesus in disguise, and to see into the realm of the heart.

EVALUATION

DAY 1	
DAY 2	
DAY 3	
DAY 4	
DAY 5	
DAY 6	
DAY 7	
DAY 8	
DAY 9	
DAY 10	
TOTAL: (300 Possible)	

Congratulations! You have made it through the first 10 days of the journey! Now's your chance to go back and add up your scores from all your self-evaluation tests.

No matter what you scored, if you were really honest with yourself about how you measured up, you are doing an amazing job at this! Again, the goal of these self-evaluations is to help you identify the areas where you can grow in aligning your thoughts and behavior with godly standards.

1. How have the last ten days changed your thinking or behavior?

2. What is one specific area in which you want to grow over the next ten days of the journal? What is one thing you are going to do to strengthen that area?

"If you do it often, you are covering up deeper issues in your heart."
(page 89)

DAILY TRUTH
PURITY PLAN, PART 3: MASTURBATION AND INTIMACY

Though there is no explicit law about masturbation in the Bible, it's obvious that habitual masturbation is not the purpose for which God designed your sexuality. His design is all about connection.

Even on the physical level, the hormones released during sex are all designed to bond you with your sexual partner. Masturbation is actually an act of bonding with a non-partner, and this is why most people feel worse (lonelier, guiltier, and less powerful) after masturbating, instead of feeling better.

Any kind of sex that is not expressed as a total spirit, soul, and body connection between you and your wife falls short of God's best for you. Masturbation is not the best way to "relieve sexual tension" as you prepare for marriage because it trains you to move away from intimacy in order to get your sexual needs met.

Instead of seeing your single years as years of sexual frustration, embrace the idea that this is the season where you get to learn how to meet your physical, emotional, and spiritual needs through your relationship with God and with close friends. These relational skills are absolutely essential in marriage. ★

MASTURBATION MOVES YOU AWAY FROM INTIMACY...

Summary: You were designed for intimacy. Any expression of sexuality that leads you away from deeper relationship with God and your wife works against you.

SOUND WISDOM

There's more to sex than mere skin on skin. Sex is as much spiritual mystery as physical fact. As written in Scripture, "The two become one." Since we want to become spiritually one with the Master, we must not pursue the kind of sex that avoids commitment and intimacy, leaving us more lonely than ever—the kind of sex that can never "become one."

1 Corinthians 6:16a–17 MSG

Like any behavior, the real issue with masturbation is not the "fruit" but the "root." The root issue is your level of intimacy and trust with God. The goal is to learn to run to Him as your first source of intimacy and comfort. Otherwise you will inevitably set up a false comforter as an idol in your heart, which will ultimately lead you into bondage.

Every choice you make in managing your sex drive is moving you either toward or away from becoming a person who can hold up your end of a commitment in a relationship. If you want God's best, you need to remove everything that blocks you from intimacy. Shame, fear, guilt, selfishness, pride, idolatry (addiction is a form of idolatry) and self-hatred are all enemies of intimacy. Declare war on these things and invite the Holy Spirit to uproot every one of them from your heart.

REAL STORY

I remember the first time I masturbated. I was on a school trip to Germany, sharing a testosterone-charged room with my peers. We were all competing to prove that we were making it through puberty and could demonstrate our "manhood." I remember wanting to be a man and wanting not to be bullied. So I did it...and at the age of 13, that boy discovered a new drug. After I made it home, all I could think about was this overwhelming desire to get that feeling again. This became my life. Every day I wanted to wake up and feel it, and arrive home from school and feel it. It was all I could think about. I would destroy friendships with women because I would sexualize them and "use" them as fantasies for masturbation.

When I realized that I was destroying my life and future, I started to fight it, but it was harder than anything I had ever tried to do before. Then I realized, to see God, I had to look at Him. Merely turning away from my guilt and shame actually turned me away from Him. He was on the other side of the shame and guilt; I had to go through them to get to Him. The good thing was, He was trying to pull me through them too. I actively would pursue Him when I felt horny or wanted to look at porn, until the shout of the lust grew dim and the voice of the Lord grew loud. Day by day, fight by fight, I overcame it. Now I can have responsible relationships with women. I can control my sexual needs. And I am learning to understand my body, what it really wants, and how to fill it with the help of God, friends, and family.

Sam
AGE 25 ENGLAND

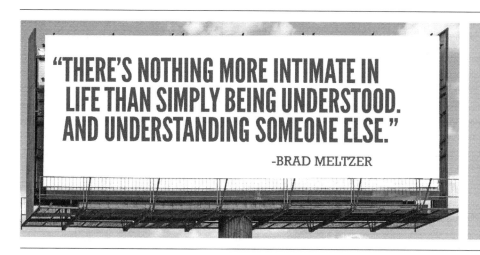

"THERE'S NOTHING MORE INTIMATE IN LIFE THAN SIMPLY BEING UNDERSTOOD. AND UNDERSTANDING SOMEONE ELSE."

-BRAD MELTZER

In a survey of 600 Christian men, 61% of married men reported that they masturbate, most of them on a weekly basis. Only 13% say they felt this is normal.

Source: http://www.blazinggrace.org

INTERACT

What is your experience with masturbation, and what is the fruit of this in your life?

When you are in pain or discomfort, whether physical, emotional, or spiritual, who or what do you look to for relief and comfort?

What is your greatest pleasure in life? Would you be willing to give it up if God asked you to in order to make room for something better He wanted to give you?

COMFORT TEST

	STRONGLY DISAGREE	MOSTLY DISAGREE	AGREE SOMEWHAT	MOSTLY AGREE	STRONGLY AGREE
When I am in discomfort and pain, I am aware that I have a choice of who or what I will look to for comfort and relief.	1	2	3	4	5
I want to look to God as my first source of comfort and intimacy.	1	2	3	4	5
I am committed to aligning my sex drive with God's ultimate design for intimacy and connection.	1	2	3	4	5
I want to know and be known in close relationships with God, friends, family, and my (future) wife.	1	2	3	4	5
I am the master of my sex drive. My sex drive does not master me.	1	2	3	4	5
I am committed to overcoming every hindrance to intimacy in my life.	1	2	3	4	5

Score:

(Note: Add up your scores after every ten days and evaluate your progress.)

ACTIVATION

Paul said, "…the Father of compassion and the God of all comfort…comforts us in all our troubles, so that we can comfort those in any trouble with the comfort we ourselves have received from God" (2 Corinthians 1:1–2 NIV). God not only wants to be your Comforter; He wants you to become a comforter for others. Look for someone today who needs comfort and ask the Lord to show you how you can offer it to them. Acts of generosity like this are powerful ways to break out of the cycles of pain and self-medicating that can lead us into the arms—and chains—of false comforters.

TALK TO GOD

Be as fully honest with God as you can be about how you are dealing with sexual frustration and other areas of discomfort in your life. Invite Him to comfort you and help you to deal with any hindrances to intimacy in your heart.

THE JEWELRY STORE

September 15

I finally got the guts to go back into the ring store. Every day since I first saw that ring I can't shake the feeling that I have to buy it. I was so scared I almost crapped my pants!! The sales lady was pretty cool...but I think she knew I was BS...ing her when I pulled out my wallet to see if I had enough money to buy it. HA! I was afraid moths were going to fly out of my wallet. It is sooooo crazy every time I stare at that ring that girl appears... (not sure if she's even real, but whatever)...I just got to have that ring.

"Accountability requires you to invite—not tolerate—input, correction, discipline, and confrontation into your life, as well as comfort and encouragement." (page 92)

DAILY TRUTH
PURITY PLAN, PART 4: BEING ACCOUNTABLE

Accountability does mean seeking out safe, trustworthy spiritual fathers and brothers who support your personal vision and standards for purity on a regular basis. These partners are there to help you walk through the practical steps of keeping that bar raised in your life. In these relationships, you should be able to be gut-honest and vulnerable about your heart and how you're doing in the battle for purity. These safe and trustworthy relationships should have the following characteristics:

1. They understand that you are on a learning journey. They do not expect perfection and they are extremely patient in helping you move forward, even when you stumble.

2. They won't disrespect you by taking control of your life in any way or by telling you what to think. They will simply offer what they know from their own experience and ask questions that help you better think for yourself.

3. They respect your relationship with the Holy Spirit, and their guidance will lead you toward deeper intimacy and trust with Him.

4. They will treat you like a prince who is destined and able to become a powerful and pure lover of God.

5. They speak about sex with honor and without shame. You should feel safe and invited to bring up any sexual questions or concerns you have.

6. They will be passionate and uncompromising about God's standards for your life. They will be unafraid to confront you, in love, with God's standard.

7. They should be free of any bondage you're dealing with. An accountability partner is not someone who struggles with the same things you do. That wouldn't be helpful! What you really need is someone who is strong and brings strength to you. ★

Summary: Accountability does not mean making other people responsible to police you or manage your relational choices—that would violate freedom and love.

SOUND WISDOM

Fools are headstrong and do what they like; wise people take advice.

Proverbs 12:15 MSG

The first section of the book of Proverbs records the wisdom Solomon received from his father, King David. A lot of parents who made sexual mistakes feel insecure about teaching their kids about sex. But David, who majorly messed up with Solomon's own mom, Bathsheba, didn't hesitate to take his son aside and say, "Hey son, let me show you how these choices will play out for you. You don't have to repeat the mistakes I made." What's the point? The relationships that will help you on your purity journey aren't necessarily with people who have done everything right, but with people who have learned lessons and aren't ashamed to share what they have learned. They will be humble enough to share their stories with you and strong enough to help you out. Your job is to be humble enough to listen to them.

REAL STORY

Part of the new way of doing life when I came to Jesus was accountability and boundaries. Accountability was basically the idea that I'm not the only person who knows what is going on in my life, and I'm responsible for my life. Boundaries meant that I protected what was valuable and important to me and others. These two ways of living became very real when I began a dating relationship. When our relationship began, we immediately found people we could talk to about our relationship and our physical boundaries so that we could be kept accountable.

On one occasion, we crossed one of the boundaries we put in place for kissing and cuddling, and soon after we felt shame for not honoring the boundary. I started crying for kissing her too much. But I knew what we had to do. We called our accountability partners and openly told them about how we crossed our kissing boundary and didn't want to hide it. We knew that if we hid it, we would give shame power over us. So we repented to God, to one another, and to our leaders. It changed our life. They met us with grace and correction that enabled us to live at a high standard of purity. We knew that we could go to them and let them know anything about our relationship and it would be safe. If we weren't accountable to someone about our boundaries, they could have been easily broken, but since someone else knew about them, we had responsibility for our lives. That responsibility matured our relationship.

Chris
AGE 25 CALIFORNIA, USA

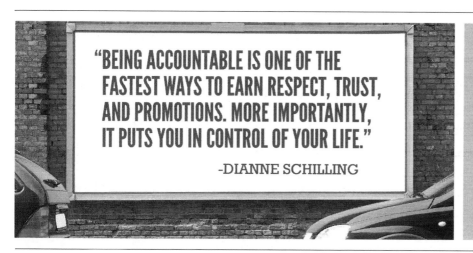

"BEING ACCOUNTABLE IS ONE OF THE FASTEST WAYS TO EARN RESPECT, TRUST, AND PROMOTIONS. MORE IMPORTANTLY, IT PUTS YOU IN CONTROL OF YOUR LIFE."

-DIANNE SCHILLING

1 out of 5 teens has not had a conversation with their parents that lasted 10 minutes in more than a month.

Source: http://www.swmihoh.org

INTERACT

Do you have a person in your life who fits the guidelines listed for accountability partners? Why or why not? Are you willing to pursue a relationship where you can be real about your purity journey?

How well do you receive input and correction? Do you seek correction when you feel like you are getting off track in some area of your life?

When you see someone you love acting below his or her standards, do you 1) get in their face, 2) blow it off, or 3) gently and lovingly confront them? Why?

ACCOUNTABILITY TEST

	STRONGLY DISAGREE	MOSTLY DISAGREE	AGREE SOMEWHAT	MOSTLY AGREE	STRONGLY AGREE
I want the input and correction of trusted friends and leaders in my life, including the areas of my sexuality and relationships.	1	2	3	4	5
I am responsible to be honest and vulnerable about what is really going on in my heart and where I am struggling.	1	2	3	4	5
I need others to support me in the battle for purity, and they need my support.	1	2	3	4	5
I have someone with whom I talk honestly about my sexuality.	1	2	3	4	5
I welcome a loving confrontation when I am, knowingly or unknowingly, making choices that compromise my identity and destiny.	1	2	3	4	5
I want to learn from the mistakes of others so I don't have to make the same mistakes myself.	1	2	3	4	5

Score:

(Note: Add up your scores after every ten days and evaluate your progress.)

ACTIVATION

If you don't have a purity accountability partner, start looking for one. If you do you have one, find one thing you can do to be more intentional about connecting with that person and sharing how you're doing in your purity journey.

TALK TO GOD

Ask God to establish you in strong, safe, and supportive relationships with brothers and fathers who are 100% with you in your purity journey.

"The war over your virginity is too vicious for you to not be proactive about it. If you fail to plan, you have planned to fail! Obviously, this means that you have to have a conversation with that person about his or her convictions before you get into a romantic relationship of any kind." (page 95–96)

DAILY TRUTH
TALKING ABOUT SEX...WITH THE OPPOSITE SEX

The idea of announcing your standards for sex to a girl you are interested in is probably a bit uncomfortable. Everything in you is trying not to scare her off. But remember, you want to scare off the girls who don't share your standards. It's enough of a challenge for two people who do share the same values to guard each other's hearts and purity as they move toward marriage. The discomfort of breaking the ice about sex is nothing compared to the crazy pressure of being with someone who doesn't share your values. And a girl who does share your values will give you major points for taking the lead in communicating your boundaries.

Remember, modesty and purity are not the same thing. The only way you can find that out is by hearing it directly from her. You want to discover whether or not she shares the same level of passion and commitment you have to honor sex. *A girl who merely respects or tolerates your values is not a good candidate for dating.*

You simply need to say, in a calm, direct way, something like this:

"I really value sex. I believe it is more than physical and it has a lot of power. I respect it so much that I think it should be protected, and I think the best protection is to keep sex in a loving, committed relationship. This is why I have made a promise to God and to myself to express my sexuality within the boundaries of marriage. I'm not interested in dating someone who doesn't share that value." ★

MODESTY AND PURITY ARE NOT THE SAME THING...

Summary: You shouldn't need to apologize for your standards or whack a girl over the head with them.

SOUND WISDOM

Be ready to speak up and tell anyone who asks why you're living the way you are, and always with the utmost courtesy. Keep a clear conscience before God so that when people throw mud at you, none of it will stick.

1 Peter 3:15 MSG

Peter told us to "be ready" to give our reasons for our choices. This means 1) we need to know why we are doing what we are doing in the first place, and 2) we need the courage and skill to explain it. There is no shame in preparing and practicing what you would say to a girl who asks you why you do what you do to protect your purity. In fact, you would be really wise to do so. Run your "speech" by your parents, youth pastor, or good guy friends and get their feedback—not only will they help you organize your thoughts; you will know that they are 100% behind you when you end up needing to respond to a girl's questions

REAL STORY

I have always had a strong desire to do this thing called "relationships" well. When I finally met my wife, I wanted nothing more than to do it in purity, freedom, and honor, and that was the resolution I made in my heart. Our first time alone, we established that we liked each other. Our next talk alone was on boundaries and how we were going to walk out our newly forming relationship. I learned from my spiritual parents that the first ingredient of many we were going to need was to honor each other's boundaries. We asked each other, "How physical should we be? Do we kiss? How do we still have healthy friendships in our lives? Who do we allow into every part of our relationship? How late should we hang out?" I felt very strong regarding how cautious we would be regarding physical touch, because I knew it was my top love language, and though I wanted her to "fill my love tank," I had already resolved that my desire for purity had to be stronger than my desire to have my love tank filled. Wonderfully, my wife had it in her heart to have our first kiss on our wedding day, and to my great delight, on our wedding day was our first kiss!

Answering the other questions required us to be really intentional. We decided that for us to have a healthy relationship we needed community, and so we made it a point to involve our close friends in our relationship. We were even intentional about hanging out with our friends on a one-on-one basis throughout our relationship because we wanted to show them that we valued their friendship within our relationship. We also had such a value for keeping each other safe. We found that being together past midnight on a consistent basis put us in a place where we were tired and it would be easier to justify lowering our standards.

It was such a joy setting boundaries first and having people in our lives to help us manage ourselves well. We had even more joy on our wedding day when we could look each other in the eyes with no regret and no mistrust because we had both honored each other's standards, even when it had been hard at times to remember the prize. Looking back on it now, I would not change a single thing about our standards and our relationship. It set us up for the most important relationship in our lives.

Rory
AGE 23 TEXAS, USA

"ANY PROBLEM, BIG OR SMALL, WITHIN A FAMILY, ALWAYS SEEMS TO START WITH BAD COMMUNICATION. SOMEONE ISN'T LISTENING."

-EMMA THOMPSON

1 in 3 girls between the ages o f 16 and 18 say sex is expected for people their age if they're in a relationship.

Source: http://www.confidencecoalition.org

INTERACT

Write out your "speech" communicating your value for sex in your own words.

What emotions and thoughts rise up in you when you think about communicating your standards for sex to a girl? Can you identify your reasons for these thoughts and feelings?

It's good to prepare your mind for any possible consequences of sharing your values for sex. What are some ways a girl might respond to your "speech" and are you prepared to face these?

VALUE COMMUNICATION
TEST

	STRONGLY DISAGREE	MOSTLY DISAGREE	AGREE SOMEWHAT	MOSTLY AGREE	STRONGLY AGREE
I always try to have a good reason for what I am doing.	1	2	3	4	5
My value for sex is based on love and respect for its divine design, not just fear of negative consequences.	1	2	3	4	5
I am passionate about purity, and I want to date a girl who shares that passion.	1	2	3	4	5
I am confident and comfortable that I can respectfully let a girl know my values and standards for my sexuality.	1	2	3	4	5
I am not afraid of being misunderstood for my values and standards, or of being pressured to change them.	1	2	3	4	5
I am comfortable asking a girl to share her values and standards for sex.	1	2	3	4	5

Score:
(Note: Add up your scores after every ten days and evaluate your progress.)

ACTIVATION

Show your "speech" to a trusted friend/accountability partner and ask for feedback.

TALK TO GOD

Ask God for courage, wisdom, and grace to know your reasons for honoring His design for your sexuality and communicating them to others.

"When all of the systems are a go, it becomes quite a feat to shut them down..." (page 97)

DAILY TRUTH
RESPECT THE POWER OF THE TURN-ON

Too many guys have ended up compromising their virtues because they didn't respect the power of the turn-on. The chemicals that flood your body when your sexual desire is aroused are designed to give you the intense focus and physical power to follow through with the act of sex. Putting a girl in situations where you have to put the brakes on while "under the influence" of these chemicals is not fun or respectful.

There is a deeper reason for avoiding the "turn on" while you're dating. As soon as you introduce physical affection of any kind into a relationship with a girl, you are greatly hindering your ability to make a reasonable judgment of her character. Her affection makes you feel loved, but that love is only one expression of the kind of love she needs to be able to provide you in a long-term relationship. If you keep the "touch benefit" out of the equation for a while, you'll get a better picture of whether she's needy, complaining, and insecure, or confident, supportive, and strong in her identity.

Consider the difference between a girl kissing you and a girl buying you some awesome music, making you cookies, or texting you a word of encouragement. Which expressions of love are going to show you her character, how well she knows you, and how much she values and respects you? Challenge yourself and your girlfriend to channel your physical attraction into these non-physical expressions as you build the foundation of your relationship. ★

AVOID THE "TURN ON" WHILE YOU ARE DATING...

Summary: You want to marry a girl you deeply respect, not just one with whom you have good chemistry.

SOUND WISDOM

Reverently honor an older woman as you would your mother, and the younger women as sisters.

I Timothy 5:2 MSG

A lot of girls today are not really helping guys to stay pure, simply by the way they dress. Some of this comes from ignorance, some from wounding, some from overt seduction, but all of it makes it hard to know where to put your eyes. It's your responsibility to let the sisters you care about and your girlfriend know how their clothing and behavior is affecting the men around them and encourage them to start thinking like a wife, not just someone "on the market." In the same way, you should be thinking of yourself as a husband, not just a hunter. Regardless of how much you want to see your girlfriend in a bikini, you need to ask yourself, 1) how will that help you protect yourself from the "turn on", and 2) how do you feel about her showing her body to a guy she's not married to yet?

REAL STORY

I have been married to my amazingly gorgeous wife for 21 months.

Before we were married, we had boundaries... but they weren't always the best. I know we could have handled some situations better. We didn't have sex, but I know we missed some opportunities for us to improve our skills in the "self control" department.

I believe that disrespecting the power of the turn on had us moving way too fast—not just physically, but emotionally as well. We rushed intimacy, and rushing didn't give us the time to mentally process our relationship. I poorly assessed the reality of the situation, and before I knew it, we were talking about marriage. But my heart and mind weren't really there yet.

We broke up for a week. It was awful, but that week off was an important "time out" in which God helped my heart to catch up to where we were pushing to go physically.

Thank God that He really spoke to me during this week. He showed me the areas in our relationship that needed to change physically and emotionally. When we got back together, our relationship was stronger than ever. We set new physical boundaries, which allowed our relationship to grow faster than our sex drives. I love my wife even more now than I did the day I married her and I am so thankful we waited until our wedding night. When our hearts were able to connect with our sex drives, fireworks happened!

Curtis
AGE 26 CANADA

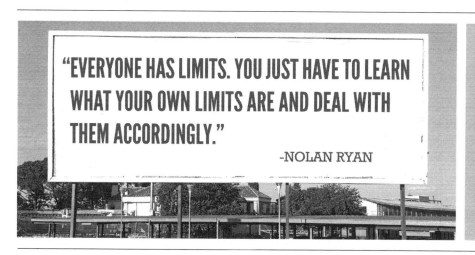

"EVERYONE HAS LIMITS. YOU JUST HAVE TO LEARN WHAT YOUR OWN LIMITS ARE AND DEAL WITH THEM ACCORDINGLY."

-NOLAN RYAN

Over 1,600 Christian guys took a survey on modesty at www.Rebelution.com. 95% agreed that modesty is an important quality to look for in a future wife. 85% agreed that bikinis are immodest and can be stumbling blocks to purity.

Source: www.rebelution.com

INTERACT

What turns you on? Do you know your limits?

Have you ever gone too far physically with a girl? What were the consequences of that choice?

How responsible do you feel to protect the purity of a girl you like or are dating, and why?

TURN ON
TEST

	STRONGLY DISAGREE	MOSTLY DISAGREE	AGREE SOMEWHAT	MOSTLY AGREE	STRONGLY AGREE
I know when I start to get turned on, and I know why.	1	2	3	4	5
I purposely avoid situations and behaviors that will turn me on.	1	2	3	4	5
I respect my own turn-on boundaries, as well as the turn-on boundaries of the person I am dating.	1	2	3	4	5
When I get into a situation where I am turned on, I know how to put on the brakes and set a limit for myself to avoid that situation in the future.	1	2	3	4	5
If a girl disrespects my boundaries, I am strong enough to confront her and enforce my boundaries.	1	2	3	4	5
If I act disrespectfully toward God, my own body, or a girl, I know how to clean up my mess and restore my standards.	1	2	3	4	5

Score:

(Note: Add up your scores after every ten days and evaluate your progress.)

ACTIVATION

Write out a statement to your girlfriend (or future girlfriend) explaining your commitment to protect her purity and honor her turn-on boundaries, and ask her to do the same for you.

TALK TO GOD

Ask God for grace and wisdom to respect the turn-on and save it for the day when you can go all the way with the woman of your dreams: your wife!

"...think about what your relationship would look like if you took God's own daughter out on a date." (page 103)

DAILY TRUTH
GOING OUT WITH A DAUGHTER OF THE KING

It's important to see yourself as a son of the King and girls as His daughters, while always keeping in mind that none of us has done anything to earn this identity or relationship before God. You didn't choose your family, and you didn't choose your spiritual family—God did. If one of your sisters is not acting godly, that doesn't erase her identity as a daughter; it just means that she is not living out of that identity.

One of our jobs as brothers and sisters is to remind each other of who we are and uphold a noble standard. This won't work with an entitlement attitude like, "Hey, I'm a prince, and I expect you to treat me like one." It will work with a responsible attitude, like, "Hey, I believe we're both valuable, and I am doing my best to carry myself like that. I hope you are too, and I hope we can agree to uphold that standard together in this relationship."

Jesus set the standard for us when He took off His royal garments, was born into poverty, washed His disciples' feet, and sacrificed His life for His family. There may be no such thing as a painless breakup, but if you and a girl agree to pursue Jesus' standard of servanthood from the beginning of your relationship, you will keep the damage to a minimum. Because you love yourself and others, you should always leave a woman better off than when you started dating. This does not mean that you have to marry her; you just have to be honoring no matter what happens! ★

REMIND EACH OTHER OF WHO YOU ARE...

Summary: Work to maintain a servant's heart as you are getting to know a girl in a dating relationship.

SOUND WISDOM

If you've gotten anything at all out of following Christ, if his love has made any difference in your life, then do me a favor: Agree with each other, love each other, be deep-spirited friends. Don't push your way to the front; don't sweet-talk your way to the top. Put yourself aside, and help others get ahead. Don't be obsessed with getting your own advantage.

Philippians 2:1–4 MSG

Here are a few questions to ask yourself in order to help maintain a servant's heart toward a girl:

- What am I attracted to in this girl? Is it just the good stuff God gave her—looks, talent, gifts? Or is it her character?

- Where is the "great" in this girl, and how can I call it out of her?

- Have I surrendered the outcome of this relationship to God and asked for Him to be glorified through it?

- Am I honestly trying to serve this girl however God is asking me to and leaving the results to Him, or am I pressuring her to change or act in a certain way?

REAL STORY

In times past, going out with a daughter of the King would have been a daunting prospect. It would have remained so, had I not made one important discovery: that I myself was the son of the King.

This discovery wasn't made overnight. Rather, it was perhaps the most significant milestone on a long journey. Early brokenness in my family meant I had isolated my heart from outside influences, whether good or bad. I did this to protect myself from further pain, but in doing so I became an orphan, independent in spirit. God had positioned fathers and mothers in my life, but the disposition of my heart rendered me incapable of receiving from them much needed love and affirmation. I subsequently didn't learn that I was a son.

Devoid of any sense of identity, I was easily made to feel insecure or intimidated, especially by the King's daughters. I couldn't comprehend dating one, for it would surely become known that I had nothing to offer. It was a terrifying thought. Then I received the revelation of my identity, and I understood that acknowledging myself enabled me to accurately acknowledge and honor others. Coming to this accurate self-estimation is a necessary part of the journey that prepares a man to appropriately honor the King's daughter.

Nowadays, in keeping company with the King's daughter, my highest goal is that she would experience my honor in both word and deed, such that she would feel valued and know that she is worth being fought for and protected.

Men, take courage. You are significant, and you have something to offer the King's daughter. Dare to believe. Search it out. Papa God will meet you on that journey, as He did me.

Shaun
AGE 30 NEW ZEALAND

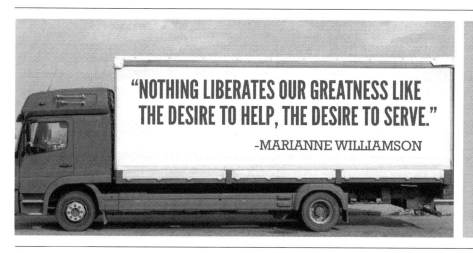

"NOTHING LIBERATES OUR GREATNESS LIKE THE DESIRE TO HELP, THE DESIRE TO SERVE."

-MARIANNE WILLIAMSON

78% of guys surveyed said they would rather be in a relationship with someone who is smart and funny than someone who is super hot.

Source: "That's What He Said," The National Campaign to Prevent Teen Pregnancy.

INTERACT

How should remembering that a girl is a daughter of the King affect your attitude and behavior in a dating relationship?

How should remembering that you are a son of the King affect your attitude and behavior in a dating relationship?

How could the goal of serving a girl help to do battle against your fears in a relationship?

SERVICE TEST

	STRONGLY DISAGREE	MOSTLY DISAGREE	AGREE SOMEWHAT	MOSTLY AGREE	STRONGLY AGREE
I am a son of the King, and I am learning to carry myself like one.	1	2	3	4	5
I endeavor to think of and treat girls like daughters of the King.	1	2	3	4	5
Humility and service are the truest expressions of royalty.	1	2	3	4	5
When I am convicted of acting beneath my identity as a son of the King, I don't beat myself up. I go boldly before my Father's throne to receive His mercy and be restored to my true identity.	1	2	3	4	5
I recognize that fear is the enemy of love and relationships, and it is my goal to overcome this enemy in my life.	1	2	3	4	5
I look for the best in people around me and call it out of them.	1	2	3	4	5

Score:

(Note: Add up your scores after every ten days and evaluate your progress.)

ACTIVATION

What is one thing you can do to serve your girlfriend or another daughter of the King today? Once you know what it is, go for it!

TALK TO GOD

Ask Jesus to give you a deeper revelation of how to walk as a son of the King like He does, and a revelation of how you can serve daughters of the King without fear.

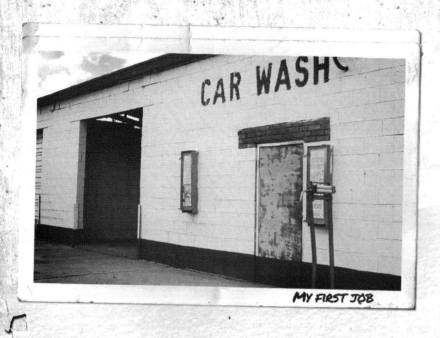

MY FIRST JOB

OCTOBER 21

I finally got a job! I beat the pavement for a month looking for work. Everybody wants you to have experience, but nobody wants to give you a job so you can get experience! How the heck are you supposed to get experience unless those bozos give you a chance? Totally frustrating! Henry talked to his boss and got me on at the carwash. It's cool...not exactly a career opportunity, but at least I can make some green to buy that ring...lol! Maybe I should become a famous Rapper or something....

$ $ $ $

"...in a relationship, any cracks in your foundation will be magnified and exposed by the pressure of another person standing on the foundation of your life." (page 103)

DAILY TRUTH
DO I HAVE CRACKS IN MY FOUNDATION?

We all have limits and breaking points that the stresses of life make apparent. Even the healthiest person gets sick, tired, hungry, lonely, and anxious. The difference between a healthy person and an unhealthy person is that it takes much more stress to get him to his breaking point, and much less time for him to bounce back from that point when he reaches it. Also, a healthy person knows how to respond to pressure, rather than react to it. When he feels angry or apathetic, he doesn't take it out on someone. He sits back and goes, "This is not my normal state. When did I eat last? What is stressing me out?" Once he figures out what is disrupting his "normal," he finds a way to fix the problem and moves on.

Unhealthy people have cracks in their foundation and they usually get stuck in unhealthy cycles. They have wounds in their heart that never heal, because they have believed lies that lead them to keep reacting negatively to their pain. For example, a guy whose father criticized him harshly believes the lie that he is a failure. As a result, he takes the safe road and avoids risking failure at all costs. Then, when a girl comes along and actually believes that he is capable of greatness, he has a hard time receiving her encouragement—he actually hears it as more criticism. He has to choose to heal the crack in his foundation or push her away. ★

HEAL THE CRACKS IN YOUR FOUNDATION...

Summary: When the stress of a relationship brings you to a breaking point, find out if you are reacting from a place of wounding.

SOUND WISDOM

A word out of your mouth may seem of no account, but it can accomplish nearly anything—or destroy it! It only takes a spark to set off a forest fire. A careless or wrongly placed word out of your mouth can do that. By our speech we can ruin the world, turn harmony to chaos, throw mud on a reputation, send the whole world up in smoke and go up in smoke with it...

James 3:5–6 MSG

Perhaps you have heard the phrase, "Hurt people hurt people." As you and a girl get to know each other and uncover places of wounding in your lives, it's easy to react in unhealthy ways that can cause even more hurt. You can save yourself from this unnecessary pain by setting a goal to 1) avoid disrespectful conversations and 2) have respectful, honest conversations.

When you start letting emotions like fear and anger overpower what you are saying, decide to walk away until you're in a place where you can get to the bottom of your hurt. Or, if you tend to shut down and bottle up your pain rather than talk about it, challenge yourself to speak up and be vulnerable. All you really need to say is, "Ouch. That hurts." How she responds to your pain will tell you a lot about how healthy she is.

REAL STORY

In my first relationship, we were both young and had few tools for communicating our feelings and needs in a relationship. I would make jokes with her like I would with my guy friends, and she would react to them, though she didn't talk to me about how I made her feel. Similarly, I would never say how uncomfortable or hurt conversations or actions made me feel. This led to majorly misunderstood actions and reactions. One day, I blew up after bottling my emotions and lashed out at her. The relationship was over, all because we couldn't communicate about our own foundations, what we needed to work through, and where we needed help and understanding.

I am now with my perfect match, the woman of my dreams. She is gorgeous, powerful, God-fearing, and she completely loves me. However, we do have problems. We both have a history, we both have things that are not normal to each other, and things that are just not "okay" in general. But we came into the relationship saying, "Okay, I am not perfect, but I will be the best 'me' with your help." We have managed to work through things with communication. We know we don't need to react, but to communicate, understand each other's hearts, and grow together. We love each other unconditionally.

Samuel
AGE 25 ENGLAND

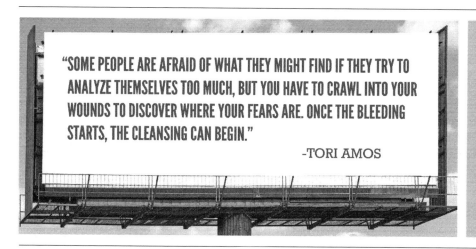

"SOME PEOPLE ARE AFRAID OF WHAT THEY MIGHT FIND IF THEY TRY TO ANALYZE THEMSELVES TOO MUCH, BUT YOU HAVE TO CRAWL INTO YOUR WOUNDS TO DISCOVER WHERE YOUR FEARS ARE. ONCE THE BLEEDING STARTS, THE CLEANSING CAN BEGIN."

-TORI AMOS

Waiting to have sex leads teens to feel like they are in control of their relationships, and are behaving consistently with their moral or religious beliefs.

Source: "Virginity and the First Time," Henry J. Kaiser Foundation.

INTERACT

1. Would you say that you respond to stresses in your life in a healthy way? Why or why not?

2. Have you ever reacted negatively to pain or stress and caused more damage in your life? Give an example.

3. Can you tell the difference between someone who is causing a wound in your life and someone who simply happens to put pressure on a place of wounding that already exists in your heart?

FOUNDATION TEST

	STRONGLY DISAGREE	MOSTLY DISAGREE	AGREE SOMEWHAT	MOSTLY AGREE	STRONGLY AGREE
I know the difference between healthy and unhealthy responses to stress.	1	2	3	4	5
It is my goal to respond proactively to pain and stress, rather than react negatively to them.	1	2	3	4	5
I am aware of the primary areas of wounding in my heart and I am pursuing healing and restoration in those areas.	1	2	3	4	5
I try to avoid disrespectful conversations and practice respectful conversations.	1	2	3	4	5
When someone hurts me, I can say "Ouch" without retaliating.	1	2	3	4	5
I want to learn where I have "cracks in my foundation" so that I can be healed and strengthened.	1	2	3	4	5

Score:

(Note: Add up your scores after every ten days and evaluate your progress.)

ACTIVATION

What is one way you could respond to stress in a more healthy way?

What can you do today to begin making this a habit in your life?

TALK TO GOD

Invite the Holy Spirit to reveal any cracks in your foundation—lies you are believing, unhealthy patterns of dealing with stress and pain, wounds in your heart, etc.

Ask Him to lead you into healing and health.

"…the more you know and understand your own needs and desires, the better you will be at discovering what you are looking for in a relationship with another person." (page 105)

DAILY TRUTH
GETTING TO KNOW YOURSELF

It's worth taking the time to get to know yourself in the following areas if you want to successfully recognize a woman who fits you:

- What are your goals for your health, finances, career, family, faith, and relationships?
- What are the unique demands of your career/ calling?
- What is your personality type?
- What is your primary love language(s)?
- What are your strengths and weaknesses?

There are several books and resources available today to help you learn more about yourself. *StrengthsFinder 2.0*, by Tom Rath, can help you discover what you're naturally gifted at. *The 5 Love Languages*, by Gary Chapman, will help you understand how you receive love. *The Supernatural Ways of Royalty*, by Kris Vallotton, is a great resource for helping you to find your true identity as a son of God. A teaching called "Intimacy" by Jason Vallotton will show you how to connect to your heart, one of the most vital parts in discovering who you are. Once you know this, all you have to do is find out who God is and you will know who you are!

Beyond what you can learn from the "experts," the best resources for helping you know yourself and the kind of woman you want are your closest friends and family members. A best friend—not just someone you hang out with, but someone who really knows you on a heart level—can help you identify key things to look for in a romantic relationship. If you don't have a best friend in your life who can give you this level of feedback, then you need to get one. ★

Summary: A strong friendship is the foundation of every strong marriage. The better friend you are now, the better friend you will be in your marriage.

SOUND WISDOM

Put your life on the line for your friends. You are my friends when you do the things I command you. I'm no longer calling you servants because servants don't understand what their master is thinking and planning. No, I've named you friends because I've let you in on everything I've heard from the Father.

John 15:13–15 MSG

Of all the "experts" and friends you should consult in getting to know yourself, the most important and obvious is God Himself. And His opinion on who you are and who you ought to be with might surprise you. If you read the stories of Gideon, Saul, Nathanael, Peter and Moses, you find they all had one thing in common; they all had an encounter in which God told them who they really were.

They thought they were nobodies—just kids, just shepherds, just fishermen, just "average Joes." God told them they were actually mighty warriors, kings, prophets, and fishers of men. God then invited them into a relationship in which He led them to become their true selves. If you seek Him, He will encounter you and lead you into the same kind of relationship with Him.

REAL STORY

What was I actually looking for in the parties, the drinking, the social drugs, the girls, the compliments? It was acceptance, approval, and a sense of belonging. I was looking in all the wrong places. What is more, I thought I needed to be perfect in order to gain acceptance—no faults, no weakness, no failures, and no fears. This led me to isolate myself so I could keep my secrets and "skeletons in the closet." I never attained my greatest desire, which was to "just be me."

A statement the Heavenly Father spoke over Jesus transformed my life: "This is My Son, whom I love and with Him I am well pleased" (Mat. 3:17). This is where Jesus found His identity, acceptance, approval, and belonging. I am a co-heir with Jesus and an heir to God. Therefore this validation is now mine. What Jesus obtained by His obedience, I received by His free gift of grace. He knew everything about me, took me as I was, and placed me in a family. As I learned dependence in Him, I stopped relying on people to make me happy and started loving them instead.

Being independent from community leads to pride and judgment. God wants us to have community (family, friends, church) where we can walk out our new life with others—a community of people who can tell you the truth in love, encourage you, and save your life from dead-end roads, a community where you can be honest, enjoy your victories, and share your defeats. Community has been a major part of my destiny being fulfilled. I am enjoying the fruit of a healthy marriage and four world-changing warriors. I have learned value, dignity, and worth for myself and others. I have learnt what it is to trust and be trusted.

The cross + community = destiny!

Richard
AGE 38 SOUTH AFRICA

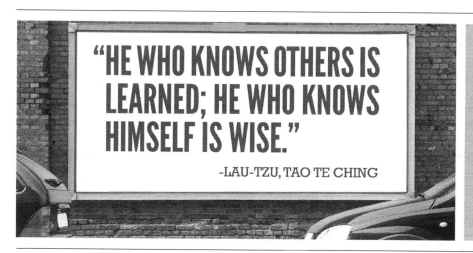

> "HE WHO KNOWS OTHERS IS LEARNED; HE WHO KNOWS HIMSELF IS WISE."
>
> -LAU-TZU, TAO TE CHING

Psychologists affirm that "other people—especially those who spend a lot of time around us and who we open up to—almost inevitably become experts on our personality."

Source: Simine Vazire, and Erika N. Carlson, "Others Sometimes Know Us Better Than We Know Ourselves."

INTERACT

How does not knowing who you are affect a relationship?

Do you have a best friend (or friends) who know you on a heart level? How has this relationship helped you to know yourself better?

Do you believe that Jesus knows the real you? Has He ever revealed something about you that you never really knew about yourself, and if so, what was it?

FRIEND TEST

	STRONGLY DISAGREE	MOSTLY DISAGREE	AGREE SOMEWHAT	MOSTLY AGREE	STRONGLY AGREE
Jesus knows me better than anyone, even better than I know myself.	1	2	3	4	5
I have friends who know my heart and invite me to be the real me.	1	2	3	4	5
I want to know who I really am so that I can share myself in a relationship and not be looking to others to define me.	1	2	3	4	5
I value the opinion of my trusted friends on who I should date.	1	2	3	4	5
I value Jesus' opinion on who I should date.	1	2	3	4	5
It's important that I find a person who knows herself and isn't going to be looking to me for identity and security.	1	2	3	4	5

Score:

(Note: Add up your scores after every ten days and evaluate your progress.)

ACTIVATION

Learn about your Love Languages! Log on to www.5lovelanguages.com/assessments/love and take a short assessment to help you understand how you receive and give love.

TALK TO GOD

Ask God to lead you into a deeper understanding of your needs and desires so that you can know yourself and what you are looking for in a romantic relationship.

"DTR is really where the 'official' pursuit of any relationship should start." (page 106)

DAILY TRUTH
SKIP THE LOVE DANCE, DO THE DTR

How do you know when you need to "define the relationship" (DTR)? When you are being intentional about the relationship, then it's time to talk about the status of the relationship. That means you have been spending time together exclusively and getting to know each other as friends—friends who have had enough time to figure out whether or not you are attracted to one another.

Take the initiative. Make sure you're in a place where you have time and the freedom to talk. Next, share what you are thinking and feeling. You can simply say, "Hey, I really like you. We are not only having fun but it feels like we have a lot of the same values. I would love to spend more time with you and have the opportunity for us to get to know each other better." If you are "just not that into her," then it's your responsibility to let her know and back off from the relationship. Hanging out a lot with a girl you're not interested in really pursuing is raising expectations in her that you do not intend to fulfill.

If you want to love a woman, you're going to have to take a risk and get to know her first. Start in a group setting until you feel comfortable hanging out one-on-one. Just remember to take it slow, knowing that you don't have to marry her in order to want to take her out and get to know her. In fact, you shouldn't know that you want to

TAKE A RISK AND GET TO KNOW HER FIRST...

marry her at this DTR point. This kind of commitment only comes with time and trust. So, take the pressure off! ★

Summary: It's not healthy for a relationship to be in a "holding pattern." If you're not moving closer together, decide what to do about it.

SOUND WISDOM

An honest answer is like a warm hug.
Proverbs 24:26 MSG

Your relationship will only be successful to the degree that you love the truth and are not afraid to tell it. The truth can sometimes hurt…but never as much as suppressing it will. Fear can keep you from facing and owning up to the truth about your feelings in a relationship—positive or negative. This will ultimately erode your character and your relationship. Even if the truth is, "I don't feel the same way about you," you should be able to say it without fear. To do anything else is actually disrespectful and unloving. Refuse to be a coward about the truth so that you don't sabotage your best relationships.

REAL STORY

There was this girl who caught my eye, but I didn't really know her. So I spent about a month hanging around her and after that I knew I was interested! Defining the relationship for me is all about knowing where my heart is in a relationship, then communicating that so we are both on the same page. In our first DTR talk I simply said, "I've had fun hanging out with you and am interested in you. I'm not ready to date just yet, but I would love to continue growing in friendship." Another month went by, and I knew I was attracted beyond just the friendship. I really liked her and wanted to connect deeper than we had been. I wanted to share more of my heart and feelings with her on a level that would not be appropriate without a deeper relational commitment. That was when I asked if I could take her out to dinner. She smiled and accepted.

At dinner, I opened up and risked a bit more. I knew I wanted to be more than just friends and get to know her on a deeper level, so I told her that. It was a little scary not knowing exactly how she would respond. She said that she had enjoyed getting to know me too, felt safe, and would like to continue getting to know me. We talked about what that looked like to us, and, in our situation, it looked like opening up to each other more and sharing deeper things (not holding hands or being very physical right away). The journey has been so fun, stress-free, and secure because we are clearly and honestly defining where we are at in each stage in our relationship. We're not playing guessing games!

Aaron
AGE 25 ILLINOIS, USA

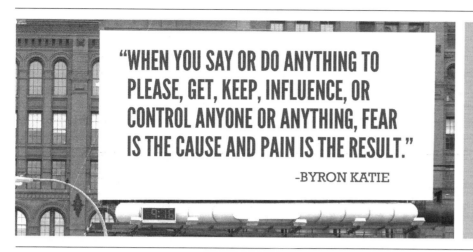

"WHEN YOU SAY OR DO ANYTHING TO PLEASE, GET, KEEP, INFLUENCE, OR CONTROL ANYONE OR ANYTHING, FEAR IS THE CAUSE AND PAIN IS THE RESULT."

-BYRON KATIE

The goal of DTR is to make sure the degree of connection matches the degree of clarity in a relationship. Boundless. org provides a DTR assessment tool to help you measure these things. You can find it here: **www.boundless.org/dtr**

Source: "Virginity and the First Time," Henry J. Kaiser Foundation.

INTERACT

You can prepare yourself to have a DTR conversation at the right time and in the right way by asking yourself these key questions before and in the beginning stages of a relationship. Write down your thoughts and make note of where you need to make some decisions:

- Am I willing to take responsibility for a friendship connection with a girl and treat her respectfully, whether or not I end up wanting to pursue a serious relationship with her?

- Am I afraid of a girl liking me more than I like her, or vice versa? What will I do if I find out our feelings are not on the same page?

- Am I willing to be intentional with a girl, both in a friendship and a serious relationship, and will I consistently be honest with her about my intentions, feelings, and expectations?

- Think: Why is it disrespectful to stay in a romantic relationship that is not moving toward a serious commitment?

DTR TEST

	STRONGLY DISAGREE	MOSTLY DISAGREE	AGREE SOMEWHAT	MOSTLY AGREE	STRONGLY AGREE
I take an exclusive friendship/dating relationship with a girl seriously. With every interaction that deepens our connection, I take stock of my feelings and the expectations we are raising in one another.	1	2	3	4	5
I want to love the truth in my relationships and be unafraid to speak it in love.	1	2	3	4	5
I am not afraid of feelings developing in a relationship with a girl, even if it turns out that we don't feel the same way about each other.	1	2	3	4	5
I want to take the lead in defining a relationship with a girl.	1	2	3	4	5
I won't allow a relationship to keep growing closer if I am "just not into" a girl.	1	2	3	4	5
I want God's best for me in a romantic relationship. If I am pretty sure that the girl I am dating is not His best, I won't disrespect her by staying in the relationship.	1	2	3	4	5

Score:

(Note: Add up your scores after every ten days and evaluate your progress.)

ACTIVATION

Practice being intentional in a relationship today, whether romantic or not. Tell your mother you love her. Buy coffee for a friend. Hug your dad or your brother. Don't take anyone in your life for granted.

TALK TO GOD

Ask God for wisdom and strength to remain honest and intentional in your dating relationship.

Ask Him for discernment to know your feelings and courage to communicate them without fear.

All too often, we use our intimacy to build connection and relationship instead of allowing the foundation of trust to build our intimacy." (page 109)

DAILY TRUTH
LAYING THE FOUNDATION OF TRUST

If someone walked up to you and said, "Hey, I want to give you a million dollars," what would you think? You'd probably want to know what the catch was, right? People do not usually give expensive things to people they don't know and trust, and for a good reason. In the same way, intimacy is too valuable to give away to someone you are not sure you can trust. This goes back to the lesson, "Your intimacy level should match your level of commitment." Focus on building the relationship on trust, and as that grows, your intimacy will naturally grow.

In order for trust to grow in a relationship, there has to be respect and honor for each other's needs. Respect and honor should guide the pace at which you get to know each other. When this happens, both people involved feel powerful and free. Powerful and free people naturally build trust.

You also need to pay attention to her character and see how she handles the things entrusted to her.

Character is revealed in the little things, so don't ignore it when she makes a critical or disrespectful remark, or is quick to get annoyed or anxious. Definitely do not blow off occasions in which she lets the bar slip in honoring your standards in the relationship! She may not have bad motives for acting in these ways, but they can show you where she is in her character growth. Be honest with her by letting her know how you feel and what you need in order to feel safe. ★

RESPECT AND HONOR EACH OTHER'S NEEDS...

Summary: As you seek to learn the truth of a girl's character, live up to your own high expectations for her.

SOUND WISDOM

If you're honest in small things, you'll be honest in big things; If you're a crook in small things, you'll be a crook in big things. If you're not honest in small jobs, who will put you in charge of the store?

Luke 16:10–12 MSG

Jesus has given you His entire Kingdom. However, He entrusts it to you little by little as you demonstrate faithfulness with the measure you currently have. Jesus is fully aware that you have to grow in holding up your end of the relationship and partnership with Him, and that you will make mistakes. Yet He is also fully convinced that you will ultimately be successful, and for this reason, He does three things: 1) He never stops trusting you, no matter how many times you mess up, 2) He is constantly there to help and train you to handle what He has entrusted to you, and 3) He never lowers the standard He has called you to reach.

Learning to be trustworthy with the small things in your relationship with Jesus will help you to be trustworthy with the things entrusted to you and by you in your relationships with others.

REAL STORY

A while back I dated a girl who was extremely insecure and for some reason I took on the responsibility of "fixing" her. I made it my goal to make sure she knew how incredibly beautiful and lovely she was. The problem was, I was very insecure myself and we had both put each other in a place that only God should have had in our lives.

No matter how much I tried to love her, she struggled to receive it because she didn't think she was worth it. And to add to that, I had some trust issues that weren't helping matters. I recognized that there were various things damaging our connection, but I never addressed them because I was afraid of hurting her feelings. I also realized I had gotten into the relationship for completely wrong reasons. It was unhealthy, co-dependent, and smothered by insecurities. I began to build a case and get frustrated, and she didn't seem to be getting any less insecure. With insecurity comes a lack of trust. There was such a low level of trust that we didn't feel safe, which

makes sense, because when you don't know who you are, it is impossible for someone else to get to know the real you.

Trust takes time to build and should increase as the relationship progresses, but there was very little in this relationship. Not only were we individually not whole; we didn't trust one another enough to protect the other's heart. The relationship became stagnant and did not develop. For a relationship to work, you need to fully trust that you are seeing the real person and that you like the real them. I learned this the hard way by entering a relationship with little trust already built. Since learning my identity, not taking on other people's responsibilities, and choosing to trust, my life looks, and is, so much healthier!

James
AGE 24 CALIFORNIA, USA

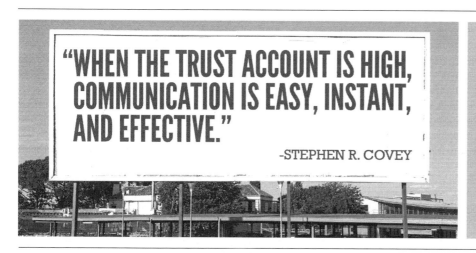

"WHEN THE TRUST ACCOUNT IS HIGH, COMMUNICATION IS EASY, INSTANT, AND EFFECTIVE."

-STEPHEN R. COVEY

More than nine in 10 teenagers note that abstaining from sexual activity in high school results in having respect for yourself and enjoying the respect of your family.

Source: http://d1025403.site.myhosting.com/files.
listen.org/Facts.htm, Accessed April 27, 2012.

INTERACT

What do you need to do to show a girl that you can be trusted with what she shares with you?

How does she need to show you that she can be trusted with what you share with her?

What does it mean to be faithful in the little things? What are some of the little things that you need to find out about a girl in order to make sure you share the same character standards?

Jesus was not ignorant of His disciples' character. He knew their weaknesses, and even knew they would betray and abandon Him, but He still trusted them. Why is it important to be able to know the full truth of a girl's character, including her areas of weakness and wounding, and yet still extend trust to her in a relationship?

TRUST TEST

	STRONGLY DISAGREE	MOSTLY DISAGREE	AGREE SOMEWHAT	MOSTLY AGREE	STRONGLY AGREE
It's really important for me to find out if a girl I'm dating is trustworthy.	1	2	3	4	5
It's really important for me to show a girl I'm dating that I am trustworthy.	1	2	3	4	5
True character is seen in the "little things."	1	2	3	4	5
I want to keep my eyes open about where I am in my character growth.	1	2	3	4	5
I want to be able to extend trust, and keep extending trust, to someone I love, even when they mishandle what I have given them.	1	2	3	4	5
I want to be a trustworthy man who can handle and protect a woman's heart and invite her to be fully known, flaws and all.	1	2	3	4	5

Score:

(Note: Add up your scores after every ten days and evaluate your progress.)

ACTIVATION

Choose one of the "little things" God has asked you to be faithful with and ask yourself what you can do today to strengthen your faithfulness in that area.

TALK TO GOD

Thank Jesus for consistently extending trust to you, no matter how many times you fail.

Ask Him to lead you into being a man who can trust a woman like Jesus trusts you.

THE BARRACKS

July

It's 4am and I am in the freaking laundry room washing clothes!!! What happened to the days when "carefree" was in my vocabulary? This place is anything but that...the sergeant is a complete idiot! I swear, sometimes I want to punch that guy in the face. He was screaming at us like some kind of freak show, all while throwing our lockers on the floor. I looked up just in time to see the sock I had my ring stashed in fall right at his feet. Perfect! I mean what are the chances? Then sergeant freak show made me pick it up so he could smell it... On a good note, I'm glad it wasn't my underwear he probably would have Court Marshaled me! Thank God for duct tape...it's like the 8th wonder of the world...

"By talking through each step and sharing your needs and desires,
you are creating an environment of trust where intimacy can flourish."
(page 110)

DAILY TRUTH
REAL TALK

Communication in a relationship is a skill—an art that you must learn and perfect. Always remember that your job is basically twofold. It's your job to let the other person know what you are thinking, feeling and needing. And it's your job to listen well to her when she is doing the same for you. It is not your job to read her mind; neither is it her job to read yours. You will get into trouble when you start assuming or expecting her to know things about you that you have not communicated to her.

There are four basic communication styles. It's important to know and understand them all:

- Aggressive: "My thoughts, feelings, and needs matter. Yours don't."

- Passive: "Your thoughts, feelings, and needs matter. Mine don't."

- Passive-Aggressive: "Your thoughts, feelings, and needs matter....(Not really!)"

- Assertive: "Your thoughts, feelings and needs matter, and so do mine."

IT'S YOUR JOB TO LISTEN WELL TO HER...

Whether you are dating anyone or not, the best time to start practicing assertive communication is now—in all of your relationships. Tolerating disrespectful communication in any person will threaten the quality of all your relationships. ★

Summary: In order to build successful communication in your dating relationship, you must cultivate a high value for your own thoughts, feelings, and needs, and for hers.

SOUND WISDOM

Counsel in the heart of man is like deep water, but a man of understanding will draw it out.

Proverbs 20:5 NKJV

The better you know your own thoughts, feelings, and needs, the better you will be able to sympathize and relate to others. But all of us need help getting to know ourselves. We need people of "understanding" who are further along in life than we are, to help us identify and put language to what's going on in our inner world. A person of understanding is a good listener—you should feel like he or she really "hears" you on a lot of levels and can even help you say what you're trying to say when you get stuck. Practice talking about your thoughts, feelings, and needs with your spiritual father or mentor. Ask them for help in expressing yourself in an assertive, respectful way. Learn by paying attention to how they communicate in their relationships. Also, the book *Boundaries* by Henry Cloud and John Townsend is a great tool for learning how to communicate the standards you have established in your life.

REAL STORY

Recently, I was in a relationship with a lovely girl. We'd been good friends for quite some time before we both decided we wanted to see if there could be something more between us. We had many wonderful moments together, but I remember one situation especially well, as it really opened my eyes to the power of communication.

I had been trying to figure out what I was feeling and what was going on in my heart. My emotions were messy and chaotic, and I felt really insecure about the whole relationship. Typically what I would do was to process through them, clear away the messiness and then share the neat and sorted thoughts in a way that didn't require any real vulnerability on my part. It always seemed like the safest and wisest way. That evening I was listening to my friend's parents share some thoughts, and they challenged me to communicate the unprocessed emotions with this girl, to share my insecurities and what was actually going on in my heart.

I remember coming home that evening and being terrified at the prospect of communicating my insecurities to my girlfriend. I was supposed to be the strong man, the one who had it all together. There wasn't supposed to be any fear.

The next morning we met, and I got to communicate what was deep inside me, even if it was fear and insecurity. When I had finished sharing, my girlfriend responded so well, encouraging me and thanking me for being honest and vulnerable. I was suddenly aware that I felt really, really good. "Why?" I wondered. I took me a second, but I realized that I felt known. It was like I had taken a picture of the inside of my heart and shown it to her. It was scary—what if she didn't like the picture? But it felt so good to allow someone to really see me.

Simply put, communication is allowing another person to see what's inside you. It can be scary, especially if we seek validation or identity from the other person, but it is vital. Without it, you can go your whole life and never be known, never feel like someone really knows who you are. I've met so many people who, out of fear of not being liked or being betrayed, put up walls and never let anyone see that picture of their inside. It's a poor substitute for real relationship.

Daniel
AGE 22 NORWAY

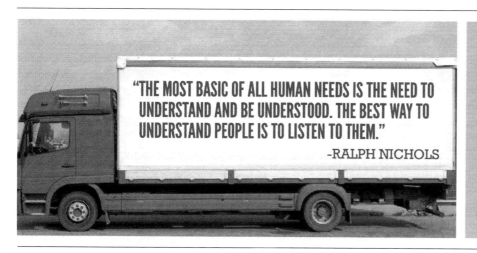

"THE MOST BASIC OF ALL HUMAN NEEDS IS THE NEED TO UNDERSTAND AND BE UNDERSTOOD. THE BEST WAY TO UNDERSTAND PEOPLE IS TO LISTEN TO THEM."

-RALPH NICHOLS

Confident individuals listen to message content better than individuals who lack confidence.

Source: http://karlamclaren.com/emotions-create-clear-communication/

INTERACT

What primary communication styles did you see modeled for you in your home? What did your upbringing teach you to believe about the value of your thoughts, feelings, and needs, and the value of others' thoughts, feelings, and needs?

What are some of the results of disrespectful conversations you have either observed or participated in?

Who in your life is a model of respectful, assertive communication? What are two things you have learned from them about healthy communication?

ASSERTIVENESS TEST

	STRONGLY DISAGREE	MOSTLY DISAGREE	AGREE SOMEWHAT	MOSTLY AGREE	STRONGLY AGREE
I have a high value for my thoughts, feelings, and needs, and I know what they are.	1	2	3	4	5
I have a high value for the thoughts, feelings and needs of others.	1	2	3	4	5
I do not expect someone, even someone close to me, to be able to read my mind. I only expect them to be accountable for the information I have communicated to them.	1	2	3	4	5
I communicate my value for a person by listening well to them and giving them my attention.	1	2	3	4	5
I seek out relationships with people of "understanding" who know how to share what's going on inside and invite me to do the same.	1	2	3	4	5
I do not participate in disrespectful conversations.	1	2	3	4	5

Score:

(Note: Add up your scores after every ten days and evaluate your progress.)

ACTIVATION

Ask a close friend if he or she thinks you are a good sharer and a good listener. Invite his or her input on how you can improve in any area.

TALK TO GOD

Often we project the communication style we grew up with on God. But God wants to have respectful conversations with you. He listens to you and values your thoughts, feelings, and needs, and wants you to do the same with Him. Invite Him to lead you into assertive communication with Him!

EVALUATION

DAY 11	
DAY 12	
DAY 13	
DAY 14	
DAY 15	
DAY 16	
DAY 17	
DAY 18	
DAY 19	
DAY 10	
TOTAL: (300 Possible)	

Congratulations! You have made it through the first 20 days of the journal. Now's your chance to go back and add up your scores from the last 10 days of your self-evaluation tests.

1. What is one way in which your thinking or behavior has changed in the last twenty days?

2. What is one specific area in which you want to grow over the next ten days of the journal? What is one thing you are going to do to strengthen that area?

"Because our emotions are so powerful, often times the decisions that we make while we are 'under the influence' are much different from the decisions we would have made while being 'sober.'" (page 111)

DAILY TRUTH
UNDER THE INFLUENCE: HANDLING STRONG EMOTIONS

Like your sex drive, your capacity to experience the full range of human emotions is a divine gift from your Creator. And like your sex drive, it is your job to manage your emotions. Some people disregard or shut down their feelings because managing them seems too difficult and scary. Others give in and let their feelings manage them. But as He does for your sex life, God wants you to have a fully developed and satisfying emotional life, where you can feel things deeply and harness the power of your feelings to act according to your virtues and godly goals.

You can, and must, learn to take your emotions "captive," just as you do with your thoughts. This holds true whether your emotions are positive or negative. Both the powerful excitement and joy of a new relationship and the powerful ache of loneliness will push you to act in ways that either honor your virtues or don't. No matter how strong the feeling may be, you always have the power to choose how you will respond to it. Relationships founded on emotions are at the mercy of emotional changes—and emotions will change. If you don't want to be an emotional rollercoaster, make sure that you decide what you're going to do with the emotions you feel.

Use the messages your emotions are communicating to help you to make decisions, but always make sure that your powers of reason and your knowledge of truth weigh in on those decisions. Don't ever let your emotions be the only thing that determines your behavior. ★

ACT ACCORDING TO YOUR VIRTUES...

Summary:
The commitments you make should be inspired by your emotions, but should also rule your emotions.

SOUND WISDOM

When [Jesus] looked out over the crowds, his heart broke. (Matthew 9:36 MSG)

When Jesus saw her sobbing and the Jews with her sobbing, a deep anger welled up within him...Now Jesus wept. (John 11:33, 35 MSG)

At that, Jesus rejoiced, exuberant in the Holy Spirit. (Luke 10:21)

Jesus felt all kinds of strong emotions—anger, grief, compassion, and joy—and expressed them with a freedom that makes most of us look like robots. But whatever "moved" Him always moved Him toward His God-given assignments and goals, not away from them. He also knew how to move consistently toward those assignments with or without the help of strong emotions. His character created safe boundaries in which He could be vulnerable to His feelings, but not ruled by them.

If you are afraid of strong emotions, Jesus wants to heal your heart and awaken your ability to feel, within the security created by the power He gives you to manage your feelings well.

REAL STORY

When I was 13 years old at youth camp I was teased by a sixteen-year-old boy. Something he said triggered me. It was like I couldn't help myself—I just lost it and punched him a few times. After doing it, I knew I shouldn't have, and we ended up being assigned a day of hauling branches at a nearby orchard to learn our lesson. It's a lesson I never forgot. I learned that expressing my anger and directing it at another person is not a good option. The reason I punched him wasn't about him, it was about me and what was going on inside of me.

Whenever anger comes up in me, I remember that taking it out on someone else won't help at all. I've only found one thing that does help, and that is turning to Father God. I tell Him what's going on with me and ask for help. And He's always there when I ask.

Another really practical tool I've found is that, as a man, I need to "fight" in some way. I have found a few sports where I can do that. While playing racquetball, I can exert myself fully and safely. If I don't play any competitive sports with other guys for a while, I have noticed that I start to get on edge. I need to get the "fight" out of my system on a consistent basis.

Chris
AGE 30 OHIO, USA

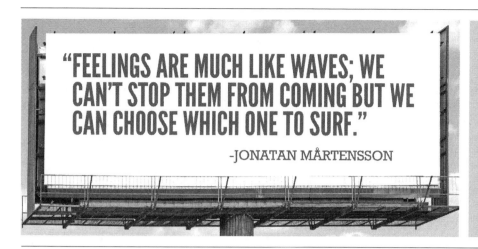

"FEELINGS ARE MUCH LIKE WAVES; WE CAN'T STOP THEM FROM COMING BUT WE CAN CHOOSE WHICH ONE TO SURF."

-JONATAN MÅRTENSSON

Without emotions, you can't think clearly, make competent decisions, or communicate.

Source: http://karlamclaren.com

INTERACT

When was the last time you experienced a strong emotion, positive or negative?

Did you, or can you, identify the cause of that emotion? What did you do about it?

Have you ever made a decision while "under the influence" of a strong emotion, and what was it?

Was this decision in line with your virtues or not?

Are you afraid of strong emotions? Why or why not?

EMOTIONS TEST

	STRONGLY DISAGREE	MOSTLY DISAGREE	AGREE SOMEWHAT	MOSTLY AGREE	STRONGLY AGREE
My capacity to experience strong emotions is a gift from God, and I am thankful for it.	1	2	3	4	5
I am responsible to manage my emotions and respond to them in ways that honor my virtues.	1	2	3	4	5
I refuse to let my emotions manage me or tell me how to make decisions.	1	2	3	4	5
I build my relationships on the foundation of my virtues, not my emotions.	1	2	3	4	5
I want to be able to feel things deeply and be moved by my emotions, like Jesus does.	1	2	3	4	5
I want to be able to follow through on my commitments, whether I feel like it or not.	1	2	3	4	5

Score:

(Note: Add up your scores after every ten days and evaluate your progress.)

ACTIVATION

Practice checking in with your emotions today. Ask yourself, "What am I feeling? Why am I feeling it? How should I respond to this?"

TALK TO GOD

Invite Jesus to lead you into aligning your emotional life with your virtues and purpose.

Ask Him to heal any places where your emotions have been shut down or out of control.

"Interdependence means that I lend my strength to help you become all that you can be, and you lend me your strength to help me become all that I was created to be." (page 114)

DAILY TRUTH
INTERDEPENDENCE

The foundation of interdependent relationships is mature love. A person with mature love is able to say with integrity, "I will love you no matter what you do." When two people are able to say this to one another, it lays the foundation for a relationship in which both are freely sending and receiving high levels of support and encouragement. This is relationship as God designed it.

OFTENTIMES WE WITHHOLD LOVE BECAUSE OF FEAR...

Most people never step fully into the incredible joy of an interdependent, life-giving relationship because they never learn to trust God in every situation. Oftentimes we withhold love, or give love with conditions, because of fear.

Realistically, because you and whomever you date and marry are in the process of developing mature love, there are going to be times where you do hurt each other.

God allows these moments where your love cannot be reciprocated to test and grow your love ★

I WILL LOVE YOU NO MATTER WHAT...

Summary: Situations that test your ability to love like God may affect your decision about who to marry, but they should never affect your commitment to pursue mature love.

SOUND WISDOM

"If someone strikes you, stand there and take it. If someone drags you into court and sues for the shirt off your back, giftwrap your best coat and make a present of it. And if someone takes unfair advantage of you, use the occasion to practice the servant life. No more tit-for-tat stuff. Live generously."

Matthew 5:39–42 MSG

You will be really smart if you look for a lady who goes the extra mile. Pay attention to how she treats those who can't repay her, or who treat her unkindly. If she shows them kindness, forgiveness and generosity in words and action, then you have evidence that she can hold up her end of an interdependent relationship.

An interdependent relationship isn't just about being able to give, though; it is equally about being able to receive. It takes strength to be vulnerable and say, "Hey, I'm (tired, hurting, weak) right now, and I need some help." A girl who "doesn't need anybody" is not ready for interdependence.

Also, regularly check in with yourself and look at whether or not you are going the extra mile in your life, or whether or not you have a hard time asking for help when you need it.

REAL STORY

Like many people, as I grew up, I looked forward to the day when I would find the woman I would marry. I was excited to love someone that deeply, but if I was honest, I was probably even more excited to feel her love for me. So often we go through life wanting to find and feel love, but now, after 10 years of marriage, I have realized there are plenty of times I don't "feel" love from my wife or for her. Yes, there are times I have found myself cleaning up the house or doing laundry with clenched teeth.

Even though I may feel hurt by my wife in some random conflict, I know one of the ways she receives love is when acts of service are done for her. So these times, more than any others, I tell myself what I will do…and that is to do the things that communicate love to her regardless of what happened. Trust me, it can feel very unfair, but then I remind myself that I chose to marry her. I chose to love her. And most of all, even though I feel hurt, scared, or angry, I will still move toward her with an act of love. I don't always do it perfectly, or even gracefully, and sometimes it takes a bit to move past something unpleasant.

In the end, though, I am learning that if I can create a safe place for my wife to know that she is loved no matter what, then she is more likely to open up and be more of the woman she is called to be. Then we both win. She wins because she feels safe in my love for her, and I win because I get to watch my lovely wife blossom more and more into all that she is designed to be. And she does the same for me. True love? It's definitely not a feeling as much as a choice. It's a stance we take from inside ourselves. The best part is the bliss we feel knowing deep inside ourselves that she knows me and I know her and that no matter what happens, we will choose to love each other through the good and the bad.

Brad
AGE 40 MICHIGAN, USA

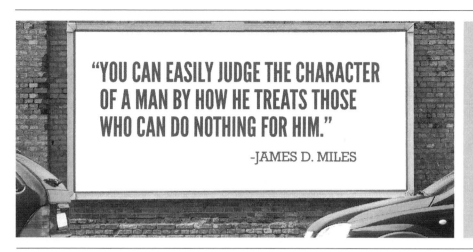

"YOU CAN EASILY JUDGE THE CHARACTER OF A MAN BY HOW HE TREATS THOSE WHO CAN DO NOTHING FOR HIM."

-JAMES D. MILES

Couples who live together are less happy than married couples and are less happy with their sex lives. In America, long-term cohabiting relationships are far rarer than successful marriages.

Source: Linda J. Waite and Maggie Gallagher, *The Case for Marriage: Why Married People are Happier, Healthier, and Better Off Financially.*

INTERACT

Why is being able to love someone who can't or doesn't love you back, and even someone who hurts you, a foundational ability for a mutual, loving, interdependent relationship?

Describe a time where you withheld love in a relationship, or someone withheld love from you, because of fear. How did this affect the relationship?

Have you ever received grace from Jesus to love someone who otherwise you could not love? How did this affect you and your relationships?

When was the last time you went the extra mile for someone? Describe what you did and how it affected your life and theirs.

MATURITY TEST

	STRONGLY DISAGREE	MOSTLY DISAGREE	AGREE SOMEWHAT	MOSTLY AGREE	STRONGLY AGREE
I believe God can help me to love someone no matter what they do.	1	2	3	4	5
I want to be really good at showing love and really good at receiving love in relationships with God and others.	1	2	3	4	5
I work on staying connected to God's eternal source of love so that I can love others without fear or conditions.	1	2	3	4	5
I check in with myself regularly to see if I am withholding love or loving with conditions because of fear.	1	2	3	4	5
I go the extra mile for others, and not for just my friends, but also for people who can't repay me.	1	2	3	4	5
I know how to offer my strength to others, and I know how to receive strength from others.	1	2	3	4	5

Score:

(Note: Add up your scores after every ten days and evaluate your progress.)

ACTIVATION

If there is any relationship in your life in which you know you are withholding love or loving with conditions, choose to show love to that person in some way today. If you are resisting someone's love and wanting to be independent and self-sufficient, choose to humble yourself and receive that person's love.

TALK TO GOD

Ask God to reveal any area of your life where you are acting dependent or independent, and to give you wisdom and strength to move toward interdependence, both in your relationship with Him and with others.

"Intimacy is so important because it's how we receive the highest level of love." (page 116)

DAILY TRUTH
INTO ME YOU SEE

Intimacy is the key ingredient to an amazing relationship. Nothing can come close to the feeling of being deeply known. Make no mistake, there are many cheap imitations of intimacy. The desire to feel connected compels people (usually altered by drugs and alcohol) to keep heading to nightclubs, sports games, or porn sites to escape their loneliness, but after each encounter the feeling passes and leaves them empty. But true intimacy is a lasting well of love you can draw from on a regular basis, and it always leaves you better and richer than before.

One thing to remember about intimacy is that it should not be built with everyone; it should only be given where there is mutual trust and respect. In order for true intimacy to happen, each party involved will have to be a powerful person with real needs and boundaries. Needs and boundaries are so amazing, because whenever you meet a person's needs or respect their boundaries, you build trust. The natural result of building trust is an increase in intimacy.

But remember, wherever fear and suspicion are allowed to influence a relationship, intimacy will dramatically decrease. It's vitally important in intimate relationships that even when you disappoint yourselves and each other—which is bound to happen—you work to believe the best about each other. ★

THERE ARE MANY CHEAP IMITATIONS OF INTIMACY...

Summary: Intimacy is the lifeblood in every flourishing relationship.

SOUND WISDOM

You know me inside and out, you hold me together, you never fail to stand me tall in your presence so I can look you in the eye.

Psalms 41:12 MSG

Intimacy with God lays the best foundation for intimacy in a romantic relationship. The more real you can be with God, who loves, desires, knows, and accepts you more than any other person ever could, the more real you can be with others. And if you can't be real with God, then you're certainly not going to be real—as real as you can and should be—with yourself and others, especially a significant other.

REAL STORY

Growing up in a dysfunctional family, I didn't have any examples of a good marriage to give me hope that I could challenge this norm. My parents divorced when I was two, and my mom and my dad soon remarried. My stepdad was physically and emotionally abusive, and my mom was too afraid to step in and rescue me. My dad and stepmom soon had children, so I always felt like a third wheel when I visited on weekends. The cycle of abuse continued until I ran away from home at age sixteen.

I met my wife a few years later in college. I had always longed for the kind of amazing marriage I saw in the movies, but after we got married, our intimacy was selfish. Thankfully, an experience with the Lord started to change all of that. On a Sunday about twenty years ago, a visiting missionary from Chile spoke at church. He opened the class by stating that he wanted to share on a topic that he was just starting to explore: romancing the heart of God. When he shared this, it felt like God shot an arrow into my heart. Romancing God's heart—what was that? This message of intimacy took me totally by surprise.

A question began to stir in my heart...Did this mean that God wanted to romance my heart, as well? Why would He want to do that? I felt perplexed, yet intrigued. Intimacy, romance, and God were words that didn't seem to fit together, especially for me as a man. Yet, as I pondered this message over time, I knew something was beginning to awaken in my heart. His love for me wasn't selfish, but life-giving. This incredible reality helped to refocus my emotional and spiritual journey, and opened the doors to intimacy with my amazing wife of twenty-four years.

Lee
AGE 46 IOWA, USA

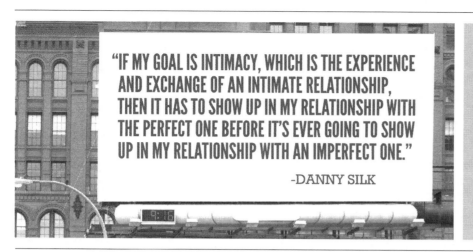

"IF MY GOAL IS INTIMACY, WHICH IS THE EXPERIENCE AND EXCHANGE OF AN INTIMATE RELATIONSHIP, THEN IT HAS TO SHOW UP IN MY RELATIONSHIP WITH THE PERFECT ONE BEFORE IT'S EVER GOING TO SHOW UP IN MY RELATIONSHIP WITH AN IMPERFECT ONE."

-DANNY SILK

Matthew Kelly, author of _The Seven Levels of Intimacy_, says we progress in letting others "see into" us by first sharing clichés (small talk), then facts, then opinions, then hopes and dreams, then feelings, then fears, failures and weaknesses, and finally, our needs.

Source: http://www.villagecounseling.net

INTERACT

Do you make your life an "open book" to God like David Did?

If so, how do you do that? If not, Why? What can you do to open up to God more fully?

Do you understand that God believes the best about you, even when you mess up? Why or why not?

How does this define what you believe about yourself and others?

What did you do the last time someone you cared about disappointed you? Did you work to rebuild trust? Why or why not?

INTIMACY TEST

	STRONGLY DISAGREE	MOSTLY DISAGREE	AGREE SOMEWHAT	MOSTLY AGREE	STRONGLY AGREE
I try to be raw and real with God about what is going on inside me.	1	2	3	4	5
I want to share everything with God, the good times and the hard times, because I love Him and He loves me.	1	2	3	4	5
I try to believe the best about myself and others.	1	2	3	4	5
I work to align my opinions of myself and others with God's opinion.	1	2	3	4	5
I am unconditionally accepted by God.	1	2	3	4	5
I want to send a message of unconditional acceptance to those around me, especially in my closest relationships.	1	2	3	4	5

Score:

(Note: Add up your scores after every ten days and evaluate your progress.)

ACTIVATION

Is there anyone in your life who you are viewing through a lens of suspicion, bitterness, or offense? Forgive them for anything they have done to hurt, betray, or disappoint you, and bless them. Ask God to heal your heart of any pain they have caused, and to help you see them through His eyes.

TALK TO GOD

Spend some time reading the Psalms today. When you find a verse that resonates with what you are going through, speak it aloud to God. Use it as a launch pad into a raw conversation with the One who is totally crazy about you and wants to lead you into intimacy with Him.

REGISTRATION STATUS FORM

United States Government
ORDER OF DEPLOYMENT TO AFGHANISTAN

DAY OF DREAD

September

Worst day of my life! Uncle Sam is sending me to Afgan...SUPER SCARED. Guys are coming home in body bags or with their legs blown off and stuff. I didn't sign up for this...I mean I joined the Reserves before all this crap hit the fan. The recruiter promised me Germany...I freakin' can't believe this. Everyone is so freaked out today...well except for a few G.I. Joe tough guys. Those jerks make me sick! They think they're bullet proof or something! If you're out there, I could use a little help!

DAY 24

"We can actually only be loved to the level that we can be hurt, so risk is part of the process." (page 116)

DAILY TRUTH
RISKING THE BREAK UP

The poet Alfred Lord Tennyson penned the famous words: "'Tis better to have loved and lost, than never to have loved at all." The power of this statement becomes clear when you understand that the consequences of not loving are more costly and destructive to you than the consequences of being hurt by love.

Not allowing yourself to love because you are trying to protect your heart from risk and vulnerability is a bad plan. God designed all human beings to love and be loved. When you withhold your love, you are aligning yourself with God's enemy.

Do you realize that you are on this planet because God Himself risked the "break up"? Just think about the risk He took with Adam and Eve. He was willing to risk the heartbreak of our betrayal and the devastation of watching the sons and daughters He loved be enslaved and brainwashed by His enemy. Then, He endured the pain of losing His only begotten Son to humiliation and death. And He did it all so that He could love us and give us the chance to love Him in return. If God says love is worth it, then you can be sure that the risks you take in loving others are worth it also. ★

GOD DESIGNED US TO LOVE & BE LOVED...

Summary: If you want to learn to love like God, you have to be willing to risk everything—just as God did to love us.

SOUND WISDOM

Don't run from suffering; embrace it. Follow me and I'll show you how. Self-help is no help at all. Self-sacrifice is the way, my way, to finding yourself, your true self. What kind of deal is it to get everything you want but lose yourself? What could you ever trade your soul for?

Matthew 16:25–26 MSG

Jesus showed us that there's only one way to love. You have to lay down your life for others. You can't just feel it or say, "I love you," you have to commit to a choice of action. When it comes to making a "romantic love" commitment in a relationship with a woman, it's vital that you are willing to walk out a consistent choice to sacrificially serve her. Obviously, arriving at the decision to make this commitment is a process that takes time.

Your mentors should be a huge part of helping you make sure you are right for one another before you take the step of saying, "I love you," so you know you are ready to back up your words. But the point is that you will never arrive at that point if you begin your relationship with the goal of protecting yourself.

REAL STORY

I was spending a lot of time with a certain girl, and was enjoying the process of getting to know her. But I came to a place where I needed to make a decision. Was I just going to enjoy this person as a friend, or was I going to take the risk to see if there was something deeper?

After meeting with a pastor, I figured out that I had a problem with committing to something that could potentially hurt me or "wasn't the best." In this conversation he asked me one question: "Is she worth the risk?" I said, "Absolutely. This girl is amazing." So I decided to put my fear aside and ask this girl to become my girlfriend.

I put my heart on the line and wholeheartedly went after this relationship, and ended up falling in love with this girl. She was amazing. She loved God, and she was beautiful and intelligent. But something was missing. She didn't feel the same way toward me. She was flattered that I was in love with her, but wasn't quite there yet. This was hard, but it was worth it to me to stay in this relationship and explore the possibilities of what this could be. We ended up having some amazing times together in the months of dating. But at the same time, I was always wondering why she didn't love me. Was I doing something wrong? Was I not good enough? What was going on? In my head, everything fit perfectly, but the problem was that I was creating a world in my head that didn't exist. I had really fallen in love with the dream of what we could be and lost track of the present. The more she tried to catch up to where I was, the more she just didn't see us getting married. She had to be honest with her feelings and break it off. This was extremely hard, because I not only had to let go of her; I had to let go of the future with her that I had created in my head.

Do I regret taking this risk and having it not work out in the end? Absolutely not. I learned so much through this process. I learned to love someone in a pure way. But I also realized that we had never really been able to be ourselves with each other. At the end of the day, though relationships do take work, you shouldn't have to work to be yourself with the person that you want to spend the rest of your life with. You should restfully be able to be yourself with this person. It was this kind of relationship I had been dreaming of all along, I now know that this is the dream God put in my heart. He wants me to be with a woman who loves me unconditionally and who I can restfully be myself with. I know without a doubt that God has someone for me that is going to blow every expectation that I have out of the water. Why? Because He's that good. He wants and has the best for us. I can never out-dream God.

Matt
AGE 21 PENNSYLVANIA, USA

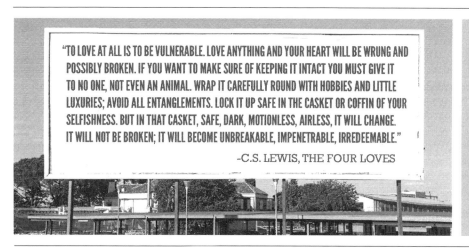

"TO LOVE AT ALL IS TO BE VULNERABLE. LOVE ANYTHING AND YOUR HEART WILL BE WRUNG AND POSSIBLY BROKEN. IF YOU WANT TO MAKE SURE OF KEEPING IT INTACT YOU MUST GIVE IT TO NO ONE, NOT EVEN AN ANIMAL. WRAP IT CAREFULLY ROUND WITH HOBBIES AND LITTLE LUXURIES; AVOID ALL ENTANGLEMENTS. LOCK IT UP SAFE IN THE CASKET OR COFFIN OF YOUR SELFISHNESS. BUT IN THAT CASKET, SAFE, DARK, MOTIONLESS, AIRLESS, IT WILL CHANGE. IT WILL NOT BE BROKEN; IT WILL BECOME UNBREAKABLE, IMPENETRABLE, IRREDEEMABLE."

-C.S. LEWIS, THE FOUR LOVES

Researcher Brené Brown, PhD found that the primary difference between people who experience deep love and belonging with others and those who struggle to experience love lies in the belief of their own worthiness. "If we want to fully experience love and belonging," she writes, "we must believe that we are worthy of love and belonging."

Source: Brené Brown, "Want to be happy? Stop trying to be perfect," CNN.

INTERACT

How can building your life around protecting yourself from pain and loss end up backfiring on you? Give an example.

Explain in your own words what Jesus meant when He said that trying to save your life would backfire, while losing your life for His sake ends up saving your life. How have you experienced this truth in your life?

How do you feel when you take a risk to pursue something you really want? Does the risk factor take away from or add to the value of what you're going after?

When you think about giving all that you are to love someone, which weighs more in your mind— the risk of heartbreak, or the prize of an amazing relationship? Why?

RISK TEST

	STRONGLY DISAGREE	MOSTLY DISAGREE	AGREE SOMEWHAT	MOSTLY AGREE	STRONGLY AGREE
Love inherently involves risk.	1	2	3	4	5
I am willing to risk the pain of heartbreak for love.	1	2	3	4	5
God says giving everything for love is worth it, and I believe Him.	1	2	3	4	5
The only way to really love God and the woman I marry is to give it all.	1	2	3	4	5
I want to overcome all fear of pain in my life.	1	2	3	4	5
I am worthy to love and be loved.	1	2	3	4	5

Score:

(Note: Add up your scores after every ten days and evaluate your progress.)

ACTIVATION

Ask yourself, "Where in my life am I not taking risks because I fear pain? What is this costing me?"

TALK TO GOD

Ask God to invite you into a deeper revelation of His value for love and why it is so worth the risk.

"The tragedy is that many of the people who get 'slimed'…
are plagued by the spirit of shame. It lies to them and tells them
that they aren't pure anymore." (page 122)

DAILY TRUTH
SHAME

Shame is "a painful feeling of humiliation or distress caused by the consciousness of wrong or foolish behavior." People can experience this painful feeling whether they are the victims of wrong behavior, or the cause of it.

Shame makes you hide, just as Adam and Eve did after they sinned. This is why many victims of rape and other kinds of abuse don't speak up about what happened to them. Rape said to them, "You have no value and no voice," and then they believe the lie that they have no value and no voice. Sadly, their prison of shame keeps the pain of their abuse alive long after their physical wounds heal, and even positions them for further abuse.

People who are hiding parts of themselves, who don't believe in their value and their voice, are bound to struggle in relationships because they never feel fully loved. A healthy relationship, particularly an intimate, romantic relationship, depends on you being able to open up all the doors to your life and say, "I'm not going to hide anything from you." If you want to have healthy relationships, you must declare war on every bit of shame attached to you regardless of

YOU MUST DECLARE WAR ON SHAME…

what you have done. Jesus doesn't make our past or present just "okay"; He makes all things new. ★

Summary:
The greatest weapon against shame is God's love for you. God's love invites you to come out of hiding and live out loud.

SOUND WISDOM

Those who look to him are radiant; their faces are never covered with shame.

Psalms 34:5 NIV

Shame is disappointment in yourself, disappointment in others, and disappointment in how your life is turning out. It can be a shock to discover what you and others are capable of, and the pain of disillusionment will fester in your heart unless you allow God to come and realign your expectations with His. Bible teacher Randall Worley once said, "It's impossible for you to disappoint God. In order to disappoint Him, you would have to do something He didn't know you were capable of doing."

He is not shocked by your or anyone else's sin; rather, He paid the whole, horrible price for your sin so that He could forgive you and restore you from every one of its effects. That price forever defined your value and removed every excuse for you to live with any kind of shame.

REAL STORY

Shame—mainly related to the area of my thoughts—was a huge part of my day-to-day reality for most of my life as a Christian. I always felt I was a messed-up person when I happened to think anything that was out of my character, whether lustful, sinful, angry or even just random, strange thoughts. I felt responsible for them and believed that they were due to something evil or wrong inside of me. The fact that I did not agree with many of my thoughts and wrestled with them inside myself made me all the more confused and ashamed to talk about them with anyone. I felt like somehow I was being two-faced—How could someone who loves God have so many ungodly thoughts?

Finally, I began to talk about some of the thoughts I was having. As I said them out loud to people who loved me and were safe, I came to realize that most of these thoughts were not even my own but were from the enemy, and that they had no power over me. And even the ones that were mine did not make me a bad person, and did not make me any further from God. I also found my close friends did not think differently about me after I shared about my thoughts. This broke the heavy weight of shame off my thoughts. They no longer dragged me down, and as time went on I had less and less of them.

Gabe
AGE 22 CALIFORNIA, USA

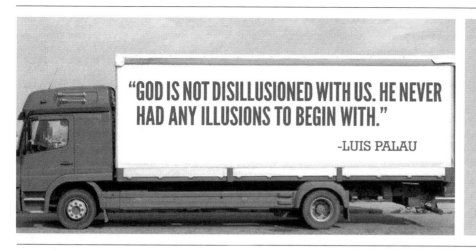

"GOD IS NOT DISILLUSIONED WITH US. HE NEVER HAD ANY ILLUSIONS TO BEGIN WITH."

-LUIS PALAU

Experts estimate that 90% of all rapes are never reported.

Source: http://www.swmihoh.org

INTERACT

Have you ever had an experience that made you feel dirty or impure? What did you do about it?

What are the messages that shame has tried to deliver to you concerning your identity, dignity and value? In contrast, what does God say about who you are and your value?

Where have you been forced to be silent in your life? Are you willing to start speaking up about these things?

What is one area of your life where your expectations of yourself need to align better with God's expectations for you?

SHAME TEST

	STRONGLY DISAGREE	MOSTLY DISAGREE	AGREE SOMEWHAT	MOSTLY AGREE	STRONGLY AGREE
My identity, value, and dignity are defined by my Father God, who knows exactly what I am capable of and is never disappointed with me.	1	2	3	4	5
God does not want me to live with any shame whatsoever, and neither do I.	1	2	3	4	5
When I get hurt, disappointed, or "slimed" by the world, I run to my Father to get cleaned off and healed.	1	2	3	4	5
I was never made to live in secret and in silence; I was made to speak up and freely share who I am.	1	2	3	4	5
When I act beneath my identity, I don't deny it or stuff it. I own up to it before God and let Him remove my shame.	1	2	3	4	5
God makes me 100% pure, inside and out, when I repent.	1	2	3	4	5

Score:

(Note: Add up your scores after every ten days and evaluate your progress.)

ACTIVATION

If you can identify any areas of shame that are still hanging on in your life (you can always recognize shame by the desire to hide those areas), then break the silence. Seek out your trusted friend/accountability partner and let your voice be heard.

TALK TO GOD

Invite God to break off any shame in your life, to heal your heart from any disappointment, and to restore your joy and confidence to live out loud!

"One thing that we all need to realize about this propaganda is that it's not really about sex or lust; it's mostly about money." (page 122)

DAILY TRUTH
THE TRUTH ABOUT PORN

Porn is virtual prostitution. Its virtual nature removes, for many, the feeling that they are using real men and women to get sexual pleasure. But this lack of feeling does not erase the fact that watching and using porn makes you complicit in a multi-billion dollar business that is profiting by turning thousands of men and women into nothing more than sex objects. And when you turn people into sex objects or anything less than complete human beings, you have initiated the slide into becoming less than human yourself. Porn will—as it has for thousands and thousands of people—destroy your soul, your family, and your life.

One of the biggest lies that keeps people from staking out a firm boundary against porn is that it isn't hurting anybody. This is simply not true. It is hurting millions of people, and there is no moral safe house for you to camp out in. If you're not against it, you are for it. Beyond that, anytime you seek any kind of sexual fulfillment outside of marriage, you are hurting yourself (see 1 Cor. 6:18). And when you hurt yourself, you cannot help but hurt everyone else who is connected to you.

If you're looking at porn, you are filling your need for true intimacy with trash. In order to break this cycle, you have to learn how to open up and let people into the depths of your heart so that you're not starving to be known. ★

IF YOU'RE NOT AGAINST IT, YOU ARE FOR IT...

Summary: The images on a screen or a page are of a real human being. She is somebody's daughter, somebody's sister. He is somebody's son, somebody's brother.

SOUND WISDOM

This is God's Message: Attend to matters of justice. Set things right between people. Rescue victims from their exploiters. Don't take advantage of the homeless, the orphans, the widows.

Jeremiah 22:3 MSG

You may have heard the saying, "The only thing necessary for evil to triumph is for good men to do nothing." In fact, good men who do nothing to stop evil are not good men at all. Good men do not stick their heads in the sand in ignorance and impotence. Instead, they face the evil in the world and ask God where they might serve best in fighting it and bringing His justice and restoration.

The fact that pornographers are using cameras and not guns does not make the destruction they are bringing into peoples lives any less real. Your enemy can take you and your generation out with any false idol. If you are not fighting to love and protect what is important to God—families established on covenant love—then you have already picked the enemy's side.

REAL STORY

I fasted and prayed for twelve years that somehow the Lord would keep me from looking at porn. I wanted Him to keep me from being tempted. That didn't happen — it would have taken some kind of weird "I'm-stuck-to-the-floor-and-can't-move-to-look-at-porn-no-matter-how-much-I-want-to-but-know-I-shouldn't-and-I-would-if-I-could-but-I'm-stuck-to-the-floor" experience, something against my will. That didn't happen either. I didn't get the impartation of holiness or the magic verse that took my sexual struggle away. I was the most spiritual person that I knew and I couldn't quit sinning, no matter how immediate and sincere my repentance was, or how noble and pure my intentions were toward everyone around me.

One month before I turned twenty-three, I found myself in a unique situation: I was sober enough to see that I was stuck, and, despite my pretensions, without any answers. I feel like my years of confused petitioning of the Lord culminated into the next season of my life. The Lord superseded my healing with His leading. I made myself a part of a group of guys who were seriously finding their purity and their freedom. They didn't do much that I thought they should, like pray and intercede. They just talked to each other. It was unbelievably uncomfortable. For the first six months, all I could talk about was how bad I'd messed up and the dirty things I was thinking. For the next six months I talked about how I was afraid and how I'd been hurt. After that, I started getting more powerful: I told people "no" when I wanted to say "no." I'd tell people when they hurt my feelings, and when I had a need that they could meet. And after three years of that, I'm somebody that I never thought I could be: someone in control of their emotions and sexuality. My sobriety is measured in months and years now instead of days or weeks, and my freedom is being measured in powerful decisions that I am learning to make.

Scott
AGE 26 KENTUCKY, USA

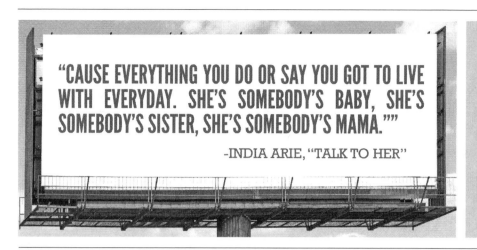

"CAUSE EVERYTHING YOU DO OR SAY YOU GOT TO LIVE WITH EVERYDAY. SHE'S SOMEBODY'S BABY, SHE'S SOMEBODY'S SISTER, SHE'S SOMEBODY'S MAMA.""

-INDIA ARIE, "TALK TO HER"

The average age of exposure to pornography on the Internet is 11 years old.

Source: http://www.xxxchurch.com/teens/stats.html

INTERACT

Jesus said that lusting after a woman you aren't married to is the same as having sex outside marriage. How do you think His words apply to lusting after the image of a woman who is not your wife?

How would you feel knowing that thousands of men and women all over the world were using a picture of your sister or mother as an object of lust?

Jesus said to treat others as you want to be treated. Would you want people taking your picture and reducing you to a mere sex object? How would you think of people's images differently if you made sure to think of them as you want to be thought of?

PORN TEST

	STRONGLY DISAGREE	MOSTLY DISAGREE	AGREE SOMEWHAT	MOSTLY AGREE	STRONGLY AGREE
I refuse to point my sexual desire toward anyone or anything except my wife.	1	2	3	4	5
When I see an image of a person, pornographic or not, I remember that this image represents a real person with a body, soul, and spirit.	1	2	3	4	5
I try to view and think of people the way I want to be viewed and thought of.	1	2	3	4	5
I refuse to turn people or their images into sex objects.	1	2	3	4	5
I refuse to think of myself merely as a sex object.	1	2	3	4	5
Using pornography has nothing to do with loving God, myself, or my wife. I refuse to partner with the porn industry.	1	2	3	4	5

Score:

(Note: Add up your scores after every ten days and evaluate your progress.)

ACTIVATION

Whenever your eyes encounter an image that you could choose to lust after, either ignore it, or pray for that person.

TALK TO GOD

Do business with God, if necessary, over any issues you have with porn and ask Him to show you what steps you need to take to begin your journey towards freedom.

Ask Him to give you His pure eyes of love and compassion toward every human image.

"...righteous people have overreacted against perversion and have made sex a secret or even a dirty act endured for the sake of bearing children." (page 123)

DAILY TRUTH
AFRAID OF THE "TALK"

What would you do if you gave your kid his first baseball bat, and he turned around and cracked one of his friends over the head with it? You basically have two options. You can either take away the bat, or show him how to use it properly. In the moment, taking the bat away may look like the safest thing to do. But this won't help him play the game of baseball.

When you really see the damage that sex outside marriage can cause in society (much worse than a crack to the head), it's understandable that some people think human beings are incapable of managing their sex drives. Therefore they believe that it would be better to just shut off that part of their lives as much as possible and never talk about it. The problem is that God doesn't agree with them. His answer to perversion is to teach us the real version, not no version. God is not ashamed to talk about sex, after all, He invented it!

God not only wants to give us the real version of sex; He wants to give us the real version of ourselves.

For unless we become who He made us to be, then we actually won't be capable of experiencing sex as He designed it. This is why, through Christ, He has given us a new nature that is capable of learning how to manage our sex drives and experience the amazing act of marital love that sex was designed to be, which is a whole lot better than baseball. Those who know and experience the real thing should not be ashamed to talk about it. ★

GOD IS NOT ASHAMED TO TALK ABOUT SEX...

Summary: What we don't talk about in the light, will be misused in the darkness.

God's attitude about the beauty of sexual intimacy in marriage is made crystal clear in the Song of Solomon. A lot of people find it hard to believe that God put this book in the Bible! This beautiful, passionate poem puts God's design for sex in marriage on display and proves once and for all that He celebrates this beautiful design and is not ashamed to talk about it. Not only that, Bible scholars agree that the Song of Solomon is a poem about marital intimacy as a metaphor of the intimacy God designed us to have with Him!

Unlike the way many Christians talk about sex (sadly), the "talk" God gives us about sex is one full of romance, passion, love, celebration, delight, and beauty. This intimacy is the prize that the pure of heart are capable of enjoying with one another.

REAL STORY

Growing up, I went through a lot of tough situations at school that led me to hold back my emotions so that I could deal with the rejection I felt. I rationalized everything and tackled all problems intellectually so that I could keep bottling up my emotions. Of course this meant that I had trouble relating to people and finding connection. In cutting myself off from the negative emotions, I had also cut off my access to joy, peace, and a lot of what God wanted to do in me through my emotions. Once I realized this, I had to face the added pressure I felt as a "half person" who wanted to act emotional even though I was not. I began to strive to feel and express emotions, but it was only a performance.

Then I had a revelation—God is not constrained by my boxes. He can use anyone, no matter how broken, which meant that He could speak to me through my mind, even if my emotions weren't all there yet. This took the pressure off how my heart "should" feel and allowed it to actually start to feel. Learning to be vulnerable enough to feel, express my emotions, and talk about them has been a gradual process requiring me to regularly take risks. But God is faithful and uses me as I am, which allows me to grow into health from a place of His plan and delight for me.

Chris
AGE 27 ENGLAND

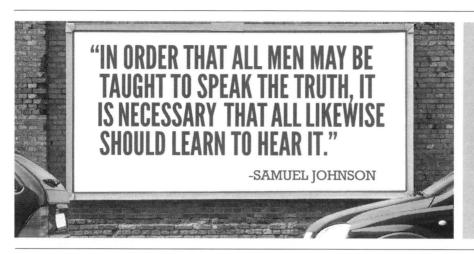

"IN ORDER THAT ALL MEN MAY BE TAUGHT TO SPEAK THE TRUTH, IT IS NECESSARY THAT ALL LIKEWISE SHOULD LEARN TO HEAR IT."

-SAMUEL JOHNSON

Teens who engage in premarital sex are likely to experience regret, guilt, lowered self-respect, fear of commitment and fears about pregnancy and STDs. They are also more likely to commit suicide.

Source: Bridget Maher, "Why Wait: The Benefits of Abstinence until Marriage."

INTERACT

What are some examples of the damage that you have seen out-of-bounds sex cause in your life or in the lives of people you know?

Has this damage created fear in you that you won't be able to manage your sex drive and make wise choices to honor God, your body, and marriage? If so, how have you responded to this fear?

Do you believe that Jesus has given you a new nature that can overcome sin and empower you to make wise choices? Do you believe that He wants you to enjoy the fullness of marriage as He designed it? How are these beliefs playing out in your thoughts and behavior?

PRUDERY TEST

	STRONGLY DISAGREE	MOSTLY DISAGREE	AGREE SOMEWHAT	MOSTLY AGREE	STRONGLY AGREE
Sexual sin has caused a lot of damage in the world, but God is still empowering those who will trust Him to practice self-control and experience sex as He designed it.	1	2	3	4	5
Sex is not dirty or shameful, but neither is it merely a physical pleasure. It is more than what religion and the world make it.	1	2	3	4	5
I want to celebrate and experience the beauty and pleasure of sex as an expression of total intimacy with my wife.	1	2	3	4	5
Praising the beauty of sexual intimacy in marriage is biblical and right.	1	2	3	4	5
I can express my desire for sexual intimacy in marriage without shame.	1	2	3	4	5
I can talk about my desire for sexual intimacy in marriage with God and trusted friends.	1	2	3	4	5

Score:

(Note: Add up your scores after every ten days and evaluate your progress.)

ACTIVATION

What do you hope to be able to tell your future children about your journey from the battlefield to the bedroom and the beauty of intimacy in marriage? Write a short letter to them explaining that "saving sex for marriage" is about a lot more than just a bunch of rules.

TALK TO GOD

Ask God to teach you how to talk about your desire for sex and marriage with freedom and without shame.

MY LIFELINE IN CHAOS

March

War is hell... it takes your innocence in trade for your insanity. I can't sleep...having nightmares...yet staying awake is borderline insane. A month ago I lost Henry from an IED. I'm not sure what or who decides who lives or dies. Is it twisted fate, or some cruel roll of the dice? Either way, thinking too much about all of this out here is sure to kill you. When the war started I duct taped the ring into my helmet. I wanted her close to me; I want to see her again like I did the first time in the window... She's become the reason that I fight to stay alive out here, my reason to hold on to sanity. Fate, if you're out there, can you lend me a hand?

"God intended sexuality to be expressed solely within the boundaries of the marriage covenant. He did this because the purpose of sex is not merely to give pleasure, but also to create families…" (page 124–125)

DAILY TRUTH
WHAT IS SEX?

Society is on a mission to prove that sex is nothing more than a physical act performed with minimal-to-no consequences. The problem is that there is no such thing as a sexual act without consequences. Sex affects your spirit, soul, and body and also the future of all your relationships. Sex does something that nothing else can; it makes two people "one flesh." You can steward and protect this God-created union, or you can neglect and destroy it. But you can't escape its existence.

Sex does something else that nothing else can—it creates children. You might think this is stating the obvious, which it is, but if you look around in this age of contraception and abortion, a lot of people have been working really hard to ignore, forget, or destroy this consequence of sex. But our biotechnology can never really erase God's biological design, and working against that design always comes at a price.

Cutting sex off from all its physical, emotional and spiritual consequences will keep you from seeing what sex really is. Accepting these consequences, however, will help you understand God's design, and how to honor it. Sex bonds you to your spouse. It makes babies and bonds you to those babies. Sex, when stewarded correctly, will lead you and your wife on a beautiful journey of the unique intimacy that makes a family. You'll do yourself a big favor by always keeping your desire for sex connected to your desire for marriage and family. ★

SEX AFFECTS YOUR SPIRIT, SOUL, AND BODY...

Summary: Sex, whether you want it to or not, connects you on every level with another person—spirit to spirit, soul to soul, and body to body.

SOUND WISDOM

Jesus answered, "Haven't you read in your Bible that the Creator originally made man and woman for each other, male and female? And because of this, a man leaves father and mother and is firmly bonded to his wife, becoming one flesh—no longer two bodies but one. Because God created this organic union of the two sexes, no one should desecrate his art by cutting them apart."

Matthew 19:4–6 MSG

Hopefully you can see by now that God doesn't want you to wait to have sex in marriage because He likes to tempt you or because He loves rules. God understands that sex creates something that should only be shared between two people that are committed to each other for life.

Without this commitment, sex is unprotected, no matter how many condoms or birth control pills are involved. And unprotected sex is hazardous to your emotional, spiritual, mental, and physical health.

REAL STORY

I've been married for four years now. For my wife and me, sex is much more than a physically pleasurable act, although it's definitely pleasurable! Before I was married, I was completely aware that sex was emotionally connecting. I didn't have sex until I was 18, but before that I watched my friends have sexual relationships and there was always intense emotions attached to it. People became possessive of each other and when one of the two parties moved on, the other always seemed angry, frustrated, or devastated. But why? It was just sex. When I did finally have sex it was physically pleasurable, but I found myself an emotional wreck. I know I'm a "guy," but I longed for more than sex. I wanted to be loved. I wanted to be close to someone and know that they wouldn't leave, but they did, and I was left feeling pain.

Since being married I've discovered a few things. First off, sex is the seal of marriage. It's what welds us together as one. It's one of the most vulnerable moments we can have with another human, especially for a woman. In sex, I am literally inside of my wife. I can't get closer than that. I look back at my friends who became possessive and devastated in relationships, and it makes sense. Time and again they used the seal of marriage outside of the long-term commitment. Their body, soul, and spirit did what they were designed to do during sex: become one. The sexual act told them they were married. When they broke up, it was like a divorce over and over again.

Sex was a good physical experience before my wife, but with my wife, it's an incredible physical, emotional, and spiritual experience. I have no fear that she's going to leave me. She chose me. She loves me for me. She's not bench-testing me to see if I would make a good sex partner in marriage. Sex outside marriage feels unsafe. You never know if the person will leave, so you don't let down your guard. You keep people at an emotional distance that feels safe, but it never is enough. In marriage, I can be me. I can be flawed. I can let down my guard. I can allow my wife closer than anyone else and because of that, sex is incredible.

Justin
AGE 29 COLORADO, USA

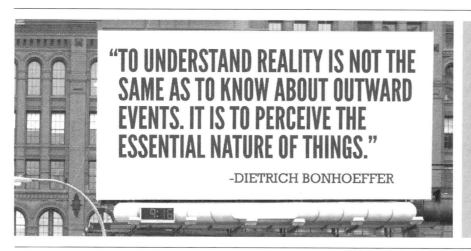

"TO UNDERSTAND REALITY IS NOT THE SAME AS TO KNOW ABOUT OUTWARD EVENTS. IT IS TO PERCEIVE THE ESSENTIAL NATURE OF THINGS."

-DIETRICH BONHOEFFER

Married men and women have more enjoyable sex, and more of it. Married couples are more satisfied with their sexual relationships than cohabiting couples.

Source: Pat Fagan, Anne Dougherty, and Miriam McElvain, "162 Reasons to Marry."

INTERACT

Describe some of the consequences that result from treating sex as something without emotional, spiritual, or relational consequences.

When you think about sex, do you think about it the context of marriage and intimacy with your wife? Why or why not?

How can you prepare now to protect the "one flesh" reality you will create with your wife?

REALITY TEST

	STRONGLY DISAGREE	MOSTLY DISAGREE	AGREE SOMEWHAT	MOSTLY AGREE	STRONGLY AGREE
I think of myself as a spirit, soul, and body, and understand that my choices involve every aspect of my being.	1	2	3	4	5
I accept that sex is a multidimensional reality that binds two people together on all levels.	1	2	3	4	5
I want to steward and protect the "one flesh" reality I create with my wife through sex.	1	2	3	4	5
I want my children to be born out of the deep love my wife and I will express to one another through sex.	1	2	3	4	5
I refuse to separate my desire for sex from my desire for marriage and family.	1	2	3	4	5
I understand that when my wife and I give our bodies to one another in marriage, we have created something permanent in God's eyes. We will no longer belong solely to ourselves; we will belong to one another.	1	2	3	4	5

Score:

(Note: Add up your scores after every ten days and evaluate your progress.)

ACTIVATION

Write a love note to your future wife about the journey of intimacy and family-making you desire to share with her.

TALK TO GOD

Ask God to show you where you can better align your desire for sex with your desire for marriage and family.

"…when a man and a woman join hearts in true, timeless love, an amazing thing happens; they invite their Eternal Father to join them in becoming a three-cord strand, an unbreakable bond rooted in celestial spheres. Two individuals become a unity. This is a mystery that cannot be explained; it can only be experienced." (page 127)

DAILY TRUTH
YADA AND THE MYSTERY OF MARRIAGE

If modern society doesn't get God's design for sex, it certainly doesn't get His design for marriage. Sadly, a lot of "religious" people have also missed the boat on both of them. They've interpreted the Bible's language of "submission" to mean "oppression" and given marriage a bad name.

But what happens when you trust God's instructions for marriage along with His instructions for sex and take off the lenses of fear and suspicion that God is a cosmic kill-joy who wants to enslave you? You will see that God designed marriage as a mini-mirror of His relationship with us, which has nothing to do with oppression, slavery, or control—quite the opposite! In this relationship, "submission" is just another word for mature, whole-hearted, unconditional love expressed through service, affection, and honor.

Ultimately, God created marriage so that we could experience love without fear! Because marriage is a lifelong commitment, it allows you to go through hard and easy times without the fear of your wife leaving you. However, if we didn't have lifelong commitments, we would all be running around with our walls up, protecting ourselves from the loss that would inevitably come when things get hard. ★

MARRIAGE IS A LIFELONG COMMITMENT...

Summary: God designed marriage as a relationship in which you are fully known because you fully love, and you fully know because you are fully loved.

SOUND WISDOM

Sexual drives are strong, but marriage is strong enough to contain them and provide for a balanced and fulfilling sexual life in a world of sexual disorder. The marriage bed must be a place of mutuality—the husband seeking to satisfy his wife, the wife seeking to satisfy her husband. Marriage is not a place to "stand up for your rights." Marriage is a decision to serve the other, whether in bed or out. 1 Corinthians 7:2–4 MSG

God wants every aspect of marriage, including sex, to be about mutuality—not mutual selfishness, upon which many relationships are based these days, but mutual love and service.

What's it like to be in a relationship where you can honestly say, "I am all about loving my wife, she is all about loving me, and we both know it"? What happens when you are free to focus on meeting her needs because you are confident that she is doing the same for you? Well, it's the kind of relationship that we all dream of—a relationship that many people have given up on because it seems too good to be true. But that is exactly the kind of relationship God wants for you and every one of His children.

REAL STORY

Growing up, when my parents would ask me a question like, "Why did you put that there?" I'd hear an attack. I also learned as a little child that when the chocolate got put out, I should shove as much as I could into my mouth or else I'd miss out. These lessons seem funny to me now, but I carried them with me into my marriage. When I married Louise, I resolved that it would be for life, and even more, that it would be better day by day. It didn't take me long to realize that the lessons I learned as a child weren't serving me well in marriage. If Louise asked me a basic question, my self-preservation instincts flared up and I would be very defensive. Later, we would talk it through and I would realize that she had just asked a perfectly normal question.

Over time, I came to really know that Louise is totally for me. That's not something she just says—she means it. As I began to discover the truth that I was safe with Louise, I stopped using "self-preservation" and started to be intentional about hearing her questions as questions rather than attacks. This has been really significant for our relationship and taken us to new levels of health in our marriage (and to be honest, with other relationships as well). I am free to concentrate on being the best husband I can be and meet all of her life needs that I can. It is a thrill to look to heaven to see how we can strengthen our marriage.

In just a few months we will have been married 12 years, and I can honestly say that I loved Louise with all my heart on the day I said "I do," and that I love her more today than ever before. And this isn't the end. God says there is even more to come.

Shane
AGE 33 AUSTRALIA

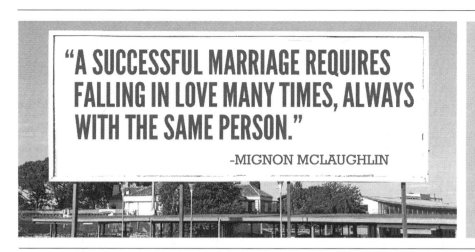

"A SUCCESSFUL MARRIAGE REQUIRES FALLING IN LOVE MANY TIMES, ALWAYS WITH THE SAME PERSON."

-MIGNON MCLAUGHLIN

Research has consistently found that married couples have higher levels of emotional and psychological well-being than singles, the divorced and cohabiting couples.

Source: Daniel Lees, "The Psychological Benefits of Marriage."

INTERACT

Do you think that you will never really know a person unless you love them? Why or why not? Do you think that a person will never really know you unless they love you? Why or why not?

Can you know and be known by God if you don't love Him? Can He know and be known by you if He doesn't love you?

What is the difference between knowing about a person and knowing them? What does it take to really know a person?

YADA TEST

	STRONGLY DISAGREE	MOSTLY DISAGREE	AGREE SOMEWHAT	MOSTLY AGREE	STRONGLY AGREE
God reveals His true self to me by loving me.	1	2	3	4	5
I reveal my true self to God by loving Him.	1	2	3	4	5
I was made to know and be known by God by loving Him and receiving His love.	1	2	3	4	5
I was made to know and be known in relationships of mutual love.	1	2	3	4	5
The only way to really know someone deeply is within a covenant relationship.	1	2	3	4	5
Loving someone is the best way to let them know me.	1	2	3	4	5

Score:

(Note: Add up your scores after every ten days and evaluate your progress.)

ACTIVATION

Is there a relationship in your life in which you wish the person knew or understood you better? Find something you can do today to show love to that person.

TALK TO GOD

Ask God to lead you far beyond knowing about Him, into truly knowing Him through His love for you.

"We are a fatherless generation because people are choosing promiscuity, cohabitation, and divorce rather than covenant relationships." (page 129–130)

DAILY TRUTH
FATHER WOUNDS AND BROKEN COVENANTS

The marriage and family landscape can look pretty bleak these days. Generally speaking, an entire generation has given up on marriage because their parents did. "After all," many of them reasoned, "if our parents couldn't stay together, what hope do we have for being able to stick it out for the long haul?" Sure enough, their fears came true—they didn't stay together, and some didn't even try.

But there is one hope. Your earthly parents may have failed to love well and honor their covenants (or make them in the first place), but your Heavenly Father has not and will not. If you tap into your divine bloodline in Christ, you will discover a rich inheritance of relational success, wisdom, and skill. You will discover an endless supply of covenant love. If you will let Him teach you to love as He loves, you can restore your family relationships to God's design. You can succeed where your parents failed.

All relational healing begins with being restored to relationship with the Father, which usually involves removing the false "father filter" you received from your earthly father so you can see who the Father really is and how He loves you. Some of the primary ways He loves you is by giving you identity, providing for you, and protecting you. As you receive His love in these areas, you will be increasingly sure of who you are, be freed from the fear of lack, and learn to rest in His safety. ★

YOU CAN SUCCEED WHERE YOUR PARENTS FAILED...

Summary: Being restored to a relationship with your Heavenly Father lays the foundation for covenant love and a healthy family.

SOUND WISDOM

God knew what he was doing from the very beginning. He decided from the outset to shape the lives of those who love him along the same lines as the life of his Son. The Son stands first in the line of humanity he restored. We see the original and intended shape of our lives there in him.

Romans 8:29 MSG

Jesus modeled relationship with the Father for us. Do you think Jesus ever wondered if His Father would provide for Him? Do you think He ever feared for His safety? The answer is no! God has given you an equal standing with His own Son, and an identical share in His inheritance. He withholds nothing from you, which means it's up to you to decide to trust Him to lead you into the fullness of life in the Father's house.

Orphans will never experience romantic relationships as God designed them. Only true sons and daughters confident in their royal position and identity will carry themselves with the grace, honor, generosity, humility, and passion required for a divine romance.

REAL STORY

I am 29 years old and have never met my biological father. He left before I was born. Although my mom married my stepdad when I was 5, a feeling of rejection scarred my heart and mind. My stepdad has gone a long way to restoring my view of good fatherhood and acceptance, but the subtle feeling of needing to prove myself to others has crept up on me from time to time, especially as I hit adult life and had children of my own. This scar of not being good enough, or needing to prove myself, had crept into my view of God the Father. I had a hard time accepting that God loves me for who I am, no matter what I do.

I have wasted a lot of time chasing God's love rather than just standing back and accepting that God knows me and loves me as I am. Becoming a father to my two boys, Alfie and Elijah, has taken my understanding of God as a father to a whole new level. My love for them has challenged my view of how God loves me and has been the final piece of healing for my previous scars.

Chris
AGE 29 ENGLAND

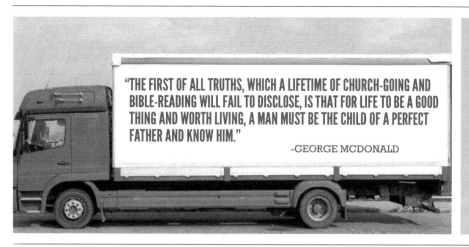

"THE FIRST OF ALL TRUTHS, WHICH A LIFETIME OF CHURCH-GOING AND BIBLE-READING WILL FAIL TO DISCLOSE, IS THAT FOR LIFE TO BE A GOOD THING AND WORTH LIVING, A MAN MUST BE THE CHILD OF A PERFECT FATHER AND KNOW HIM."

-GEORGE MCDONALD

Married parents are more encouraging and have higher expectations for their children than always-single parents, even after adjusting for intelligence and abilities.

Source: Fagan, Dougherty, McElvain, 2012.

INTERACT

Who does your earthly father say you are? Who does Father God say you are?

How did your earthly father provide for you? How does Father God provide for you?

How did your earthly father protect you? How does Father God protect you?

Do you believe that your heavenly Father wants you to have a relationship with Him just like Jesus has with Him? How can you step more fully into this relationship?

FATHER TEST

	STRONGLY DISAGREE	MOSTLY DISAGREE	AGREE SOMEWHAT	MOSTLY AGREE	STRONGLY AGREE
Jesus made a way for me to have a relationship with the Father exactly like His relationship with the Father.	1	2	3	4	5
I can trust Father God to do for me everything He does for Jesus.	1	2	3	4	5
My heavenly Father says I am His beloved son and that He is pleased with me.	1	2	3	4	5
My Father delights in protecting me, and wants me to become a strong protector like He is.	1	2	3	4	5
My Father delights in providing for me, and wants me to become a generous provider like He is.	1	2	3	4	5
My Father can teach me to learn from the mistakes of my parents and family so I can pass on a better legacy to my own kids.	1	2	3	4	5

Score:

(Note: Add up your scores after every ten days and evaluate your progress.)

ACTIVATION

If you haven't yet received healing for father wounds in your life, begin the journey now. A good place to start is by reading Experiencing the Father's Embrace *by Jack Frost.*

TALK TO GOD

Ask God to reveal His Father's heart toward you and lead you into a relationship with Him like Jesus has.

Invite Him to remove any faulty beliefs you have projected on Him from your childhood.

Ask the Holy Spirit of adoption to teach you to leave behind every bit of thinking and behavior that comes out of an orphaned heart so that you can enter into your full identity as a son.

EVALUATION

DAY 21	
DAY 22	
DAY 23	
DAY 24	
DAY 25	
DAY 26	
DAY 27	
DAY 28	
DAY 29	
DAY 30	
TOTAL: (300 Possible)	

Congratulations! You have made it through 30 days of the journal. Now's your chance to go back and add up your scores from your last 10 self-evaluation tests.

1. How have the last thirty days changed your thinking or behavior?

2. What is one specific area in which you want to grow over the next ten days of the journal? What is one thing you are going to do to strengthen that area?

"It is time to take a stand, to win the prize, to bring home the trophy—the trophy of covenant love, supernatural marriage, and a healthy family." (page 131)

DAILY TRUTH
RESTORING THE HEART OF THE FATHER

God's first instruction to Adam and Eve was to have kids and take over the world. This pretty much sums up what He is all about. He wants a royal family to share His love and rule the planet with Him. At this stage of the process, He has officially restored us through Christ to our royal identity as His sons and daughters. For the last two millennia, He has been at work spreading the "good news" of this restoration around the world, and helping all who receive the message to start living like His true children.

One of the most obvious signs that you are beginning to think and live like a son of the Father is that you begin to share His top priority, which is family. The most important thing to God, after learning to love and honor Him as your Father, is to learn to love and honor your family—past, present, and future; spiritual and natural. You may be young, but from God's perspective it's not too early to start thinking about the big picture. What kind of father do you want to be? What kind of legacy do you want to leave to your children (natural

and spiritual), and to your grandchildren?

Laying God's value for family into the foundation of your thinking will cast your life in a very particular light. As members of royal families do, you will realize that your life is part of

WHAT KIND OF FATHER DO YOU WANT TO BE?...

something much bigger—a legacy that you did not originate, but are responsible to carry and pass on to your children. ★

> **Summary:** You are called to carry the royal legacy of your heavenly family and pass it on to the next generation.

SOUND WISDOM

Listen with respect to the father who raised you, and when your mother grows old, don't neglect her. Buy truth—don't sell it for love or money; buy wisdom, buy education, buy insight. Parents rejoice when their children turn out well; wise children become proud parents. So make your father happy! Make your mother proud!

Proverbs 23:22–25 MSG

Leaving a legacy begins with honoring your parents. If you don't recognize and appreciate what you have been given, then how will you know what you have to give away?

Of course, since none of our parents are perfect, we also need to recognize the things they gave us that we don't want to pass on. But God told us to honor our parents, knowing full well they would make mistakes.

Honoring parents who were never there for you can be incredibly hard. Begin to ask God how he sees your parents and why they were unable to be there for you. Once He shows you and gives you His compassion for them, take some time to forgive them. By forgiving your parents for their mistakes, you will be in a place to honor them.

REAL STORY

Growing up, I had something some people don't ever get to experience—a father. Being a first generation Christian, my father realized he had an opportunity to change the generations to come. As I ventured from a child to a man, the role of a father played out before my eyes. Little did I know I was being given the tools needed to pass on a heritage and form a legacy for many generations to come.

Every parent wants to have polite children who eat all their food and listen, but my father showed me more than that. I was shown how to live out a personal relationship with the Lord. Being able to see the relationship my father had with the Lord spurred me to emulate that very same thing. He taught me how to pray and hear the voice of God. When I saw great accomplishments, he taught me to thank God, and when I hit those tough spots, he taught me what God's word said about it.

Now grown, I have moved out from under my father's guidance to walk as the man he trained me to be. I now have an even more intimate relationship with the Lord. As each year passes, I gain deeper understanding of how much He cares for the little things in my life, how much grace He provides, and how much He truly loves me.

Almost four years ago I became a father to my first son. Becoming a father—can anyone really be ready? I have been asked this many times. My answer is yes! This doesn't mean you're going to know how to do everything there is to do as a father. Rather, it's a state of mind. Each day I have to consciously choose to pass on the godly heritage I have been given. I have to make every effort to uphold the legacy that was passed on to me. The best part is, the opportunities that arise for me to do this for my children are endless. Even now, I am beginning to see the fruit in them. When they complete great accomplishments, we thank God. When they hit those tough times, I get to show them what God's Word says. I now understand the happiness that comes with being a father, because nothing gives me more joy than teaching my children how to pray, dream, live, take risks, and trust.

John
AGE 26 FLORIDA, USA

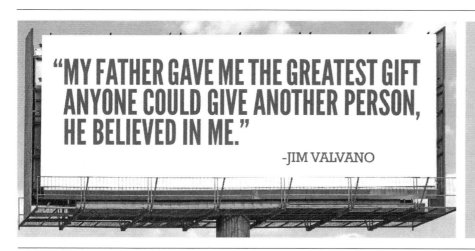

"MY FATHER GAVE ME THE GREATEST GIFT ANYONE COULD GIVE ANOTHER PERSON, HE BELIEVED IN ME."

-JIM VALVANO

The number of single dads grew 70%, and the number of households headed by single moms grew 25% in the last decade.

Source: http://www.swmihoh.org

INTERACT

Name three things your parents gave you that you want to pass on to your kids:

1)

2)

3)

Name three things you want to be able to pass on to your kids that you never got growing up:

1)

2)

3)

What are some things you can start doing now to prepare your legacy?

FAMILY
TEST

	STRONGLY DISAGREE	MOSTLY DISAGREE	AGREE SOMEWHAT	MOSTLY AGREE	STRONGLY AGREE
I am thankful for my parents and for the good things they passed on to me, even though they weren't perfect.	1	2	3	4	5
I have forgiven my parents for their mistakes.	1	2	3	4	5
God's priority is reconciling and restoring His children to Himself, and I am committed to my part in this family business.	1	2	3	4	5
I want to honor both my natural and spiritual ancestors and pass on the best of their legacy to my kids.	1	2	3	4	5
Family, both natural and spiritual, is a huge priority for me.	1	2	3	4	5
I am loyal first to God and then to the family He has called me to love.	1	2	3	4	5

Score:

(Note: Add up your scores after every ten days and evaluate your progress.)

ACTIVATION

Honor your parents today. Call them, write them, or otherwise find a way to thank them for the good things they gave you.

TALK TO GOD

Ask God to reveal to you the hidden "wells" and treasures of revelation, wisdom, testimonies, anointing, gifts, and any other valuable legacies in your family line that are laying unused.

BUNKMATE JAKE TOOK THIS

I woke up in the E.R. half dazed and disoriented from a 3-day coma. I frantically checked for all of my limbs, but quickly passed out from the pain...woke up again and I pieced together fragmented memories of how I got here. The last thing I remember was running back for my helmet. I had to go back for my helmet, for her...guess I am lucky to be alive.

Then I looked up and there she was standing beside me in a nurse's uniform...THE GIRL I SAW IN THE WINDOW!!! I completely lost it. She kept asking me questions but I couldn't even talk, I was all choked up, the words wouldn't come out. As she was leaving the room I panicked and screamed, "WILL YOU MARRY ME!" I'm such an idiot!

She just ran out and grabbed the doc...

"God is, in Himself, a relationship, an intimate exchange of love and friendship. Unlike everything else in His creation, He made humankind to relate both to Himself and to one another in this loving relationship." (page 137)

DAILY TRUTH
RELATING TO ONE ANOTHER LIKE GOD

If you study the relationships among the Persons of the Trinity in the Bible (Father, Son and the Holy Spirit), you'll discern a common theme. There is an amazing "dance" of humility and service among the Trinity. In the New Testament, Jesus takes His turn to humble Himself and serve the Father, announcing, "I have come...not to do my will but to do the will of him who sent me" (John 6:38 NIV). Then the Father turns around and exalts His Son, giving Him "the name that is above every name" (Phil. 2:9 NIV). Then the Holy Spirit serves the Father and Son by coming to rest on us, teach us adoption, and speak Christ's words to us (see Rom. 8:15, John 16:13–14). They live to love and serve one another.

This relational dynamic in the Godhead is a profound mystery, but we can see enough of it to recognize that when God invites men and women to "submit" and honor a divine order of "partnership" in marriage, He is actually inviting us into this very dynamic. He wants us to join Him in the dance of love that created, and then redeemed, the human family in the first place.

You can think of this love dynamic like a seesaw—each partner takes turns going low so that the other can be raised up. The modern world wants both partners to sit on the seesaw in perfect stillness so that they are

LOVE AND SERVE ONE ANOTHER...

always "equal." But that kind of equality destroys the whole purpose for the seesaw...and undermines the great adventure! Real love is not driven by "equality," but by thinking of others as more important than yourself (see Phil. 2–3). ★

> **Summary:** Real love is not about an equal "give and take," but about an extravagantly generous "give and receive."

SOUND WISDOM

Out of respect for Christ, be courteously reverent to one another. Wives, understand and support your husbands in ways that show your support for Christ. The husband provides leadership to his wife the way Christ does to his church, not by domineering but by cherishing. So just as the church submits to Christ as he exercises such leadership, wives should likewise submit to their husbands.

Ephesians 5:21–24 MSG

Pursuing, winning, and protecting your relationships, particularly your closest, lifelong relationships, is an art that you learn over time. You will undoubtedly fumble the ball at times, but if you get up every time and recover the goal of bringing out the best in others, your consistent expressions of love will present them with consistent invitations to receive and respond to your love. If you have chosen your relationships well, they will gladly and gratefully reciprocate your generosity and love in amazing ways!

REAL STORY

I've been married for 20 years, and for all of that time, I have always wanted the best for my wife. What loving husband wouldn't want his wife to succeed and flourish?

The breakthrough for me came when I understood the part I was to play in that. With everyday life and a growing family, I thought I was doing well…until I had the revelation that Christ's love for the Church—laying down His life for her—is the example of what my love should be for my wife. There came a point where I had to make a conscious decision to evaluate all of my choices and motivations and judge them in the context of Jesus' example.

Practically living that out looked like creating space and opportunity for her to shine by co-sharing responsibility for kids and home, adjusting my work schedule to accommodate hers, and prioritizing financially. As I endeavored to live this out, I soon came to the realization that there was a shift in my own life. In "laying my life down for my wife," I was discovering a new sense of identity and fulfillment. I felt more powerful and effective as a husband and father as I saw the joy and excitement for life rise in my wife.

The results have not always been instant, but as I continually serve, love and support her, it has contributed to her blossoming into so much more of an inspiration, friend, and lover than I ever imagined. In addition, as she lives more fully as God intended, there's been a wider, powerful impact on people outside of our family. People continually come up to me and tell me what a wonderful wife I have, and I agree, knowing that I had a part to play in that!

Anthony
AGE 41 ENGLAND

"SHARED JOY IS A DOUBLE JOY; SHARED SORROW IS HALF A SORROW."

-SWEDISH PROVERB

A high level of mutual generosity, which includes acts of service, displays of affection, and willingness to forgive faults and failings, is one of the top predictors of marital success and happiness.

Source: "When Baby Makes Three," W. Bradford Wilcox, ed.

INTERACT

What does it look like to lead someone by "going low" and serving them?

What does it look like to love a woman like Christ loves the Church?

What does it look like to love a woman like you love your own body?

SUBMISSION TEST

	STRONGLY DISAGREE	MOSTLY DISAGREE	AGREE SOMEWHAT	MOSTLY AGREE	STRONGLY AGREE
I am willing to take the lead in pursuing and serving a woman.	1	2	3	4	5
I care about being loving and generous more than I care about things being equal.	1	2	3	4	5
I want my love to bring out the best in a woman.	1	2	3	4	5
I want to consistently invite the woman I love into the "dance" by showing her love.	1	2	3	4	5
As the woman I love responds to my love, I want to receive it fully.	1	2	3	4	5
I want to care for my wife as though she were my own body.	1	2	3	4	5

Score:

(Note: Add up your scores after every ten days and evaluate your progress.)

ACTIVATION

How do you take care of your body, and how does this reflect on how you will care for a woman who becomes "one flesh" with you? Make at least one healthy choice for your body today.

TALK TO GOD

Ask Jesus to lead you into a deeper revelation of how He loves the Church (which includes you), and how you can more fully receive His love.

"Let me make it clear that men and women are different but equal.
When God created men and women, He gave them both equal authority."
(page 140)

DAILY TRUTH
CO-HEIRS TO CO-REIGN

You only have as much authority as you submit to. For example, a police officer only has authority to arrest criminals because he is under the authority of the police force, which is ultimately under the authority of the society that established it to serve and protect its members.

ULTIMATELY ALL AUTHORITY COMES FROM GOD...

Ultimately, all authority comes from God, and He has handed it off to His Son, Jesus, who announced, "All authority has been given to Me in heaven and on earth" (Mt. 28:18 NKJV). Jesus said this in order to assure us that every one of His brothers and sisters—men and women alike—are authorized to do anything He told us to do.

He has restored us to equal authority, but the real question is whether we will learn to walk in that authority and do what He has commissioned us to do. Only by coming under His authority do we truly have His authority. ★

YOU ONLY HAVE AS MUCH AUTHORITY AS YOU SUBMIT TO...

Summary: When we recognize Christ's authority on another person, we position ourselves to receive the benefit that person will pass on to us from Christ Himself.

SOUND WISDOM

All actual authority stems from Christ. In a marriage relationship, there is authority from Christ to husband, and from husband to wife. The authority of Christ is the authority of God.

1 Corinthians 11:2–3 MSG

So what does all this authority stuff have to do with marriage? Everything! Marriage is a relationship between two people who are both called to walk in and under authority before God. Always remember that a husband must be under the authority of Christ to have authority in his marriage. Then, like Christ, he must lay down his life to empower his wife.

Whenever the husband uses his authority to oppress or reduce his wife instead of empowering her, he has lost sight of his role as a servant leader. Powerful, godly men use their position to invite their wives to sit right next to them on the seat of authority.

REAL STORY

Submission...for me as a man, it felt funny, weird even, to think that I needed to submit. It's not until recently that I have pieced together the reality that my ability to love my wife is directly connected to my ability to submit to love. Let me explain. There's not one man who, while in the process of getting married, says, "You know what, I really don't want to love this woman...I think I'll just get married and figure out ways not to love her." Of course not! We got married and said, "I want to love this woman for the rest of my life." We embark on a journey to love her well.

For me, I have definitely been on a journey to discover what it means to truly love. Sometimes I laugh when I hear the famous scripture that all men hear in regards to marriage: "Love your wife as Christ loved the church." I know what that means, but what does that really mean? At times I feel like I am Indiana Jones hunting for a priceless item with a treasure map that I am trying to make sense of. This is no small task...unconditional love is no small order! But this is the key I stumbled upon: I have learned that in order to fully express love, I must fully submit to love.

You see, God is love, so when I submit to love, I'm submitting to God. When I'm in a place of submission I willingly forfeit my rights for the common good. I willingly give up my way to forge a new way with my wife; I give up the "I" for a "We". I have found that my primary role as a man and as a husband is to submit to love so that I can embody love and display its fullness to my wife. This is why I say that my ability to fully love my wife is directly connected to my ability to submit to Love Himself.

Kyle
AGE 26 CALIFORNIA, USA

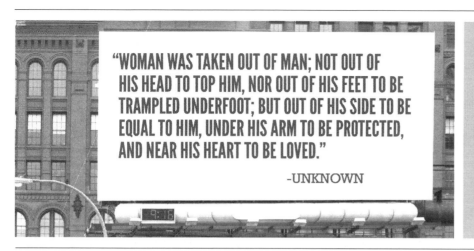

"WOMAN WAS TAKEN OUT OF MAN; NOT OUT OF HIS HEAD TO TOP HIM, NOR OUT OF HIS FEET TO BE TRAMPLED UNDERFOOT; BUT OUT OF HIS SIDE TO BE EQUAL TO HIM, UNDER HIS ARM TO BE PROTECTED, AND NEAR HIS HEART TO BE LOVED."

-UNKNOWN

Couples with high levels of commitment, who see their relationship in terms of "we" versus "me," are much more likely to report being "very happy" in their marriages.

Source: "When Baby Makes Three," 42–43.

INTERACT

Why is it so important for *a person in authority* to constantly stay aware that he or she is *under authority*? What attitude should this awareness create?

Why is it important for a person under authority to constantly stay aware that he or she has authority? What attitude should this awareness create?

If you only have as much authority as you submit to, what does the level of authority you are currently walking in as a Christian say about how fully you have submitted to Christ's authority?

AUTHORITY TEST

	STRONGLY DISAGREE	MOSTLY DISAGREE	AGREE SOMEWHAT	MOSTLY AGREE	STRONGLY AGREE
There is no authority without submission to authority.	1	2	3	4	5
All authority ultimately comes from God.	1	2	3	4	5
A husband and wife who both submit themselves to Christ, and then to one another, have equal authority.	1	2	3	4	5
Carrying authority in my marriage looks like laying down my life for my wife.	1	2	3	4	5
I am willing to be the leader in my marriage—a leader who is led by Christ, and does my best to lead like He does.	1	2	3	4	5
God created men and women as co-heirs to co-reign on the planet, and we should honor and treat one another accordingly.	1	2	3	4	5

Score:

(Note: Add up your scores after every ten days and evaluate your progress.)

ACTIVATION

Read the story of Jesus and the centurion in Luke 7:3–10. What can this teach you about how authority works?

TALK TO GOD

Ask God to lead you to walk in greater authority as you submit to His authority.

Ask Him to deepen your understanding of how He created men and women to walk in authority together.

"...God made us different because we needed suitable help."
(page 141)

DAILY TRUTH
OPPOSITES ATTRACT

It's one thing to notice and admit that there are differences between men and women. It's quite another to recognize that we need these differences.

WE NEED OUR DIFFERENCES... And it's a further step to recognize that our differences will only fulfill each other's needs as we freely invite and encourage each other to be fully ourselves as men and women. We move toward getting our needs met by loving and celebrating all that is "woman" and all that is "man" according to God's design.

Most men have been attacked in the area of their manhood and in their view of women, which has ultimately infected their trust in God. If not dealt with, these attacks can plant lies in your heart that will keep you from honoring and celebrating our God-given differences. And guess where these attacks come from? Our enemy, who works on all fronts to destroy the thing God cares about most: His family and our relationships. ★

BE FULLY YOURSELF!...

Summary: It's time for the battle of the sexes to end, and for us to unite against our common enemy.

SOUND WISDOM

Your body has many parts—limbs, organs, cells—but no matter how many parts you can name, you're still one body. It's exactly the same with Christ...I also want you to think about how this keeps your significance from getting blown up into self-importance. For no matter how significant you are, it is only because of what you are a part of...

1 Corinthians 12:13–14, 19 MSG

There is a big difference between human stereotypes and God's design. It's good to not let the world define you, but if you don't embrace God's intention for your masculinity, you will be working against your divine design. Men come in all shapes and sizes, but God designed all men to be protectors and providers. Women have been designed as nurturers and comforters.

These qualities can take on different forms and expressions in individual relationships, but the point here is that your unique qualities were meant to deepen your connections with women. In order for your distinctions to have a positive effect in your relationships with women, you must understand, value, and embrace your divine differences. When you insist that women think like men or you despise their unique role, you begin to destroy your relationship with them.

REAL STORY

I was raised in a man's world where men dominated women in all areas, especially in the church. In my conservative, evangelical background, women's roles were confined to wearing head coverings, teaching children's Sunday school, and ministering to each other when men weren't around. They were never allowed in leadership, and were forbidden from speaking out loud in church, not even to pray.

Then I married Holly, a gorgeous, well-educated professional, and my world was turned upside down. I tried to dominate her and make all the decisions because I had been taught that the man was the head and the woman had to submit to him, not realizing that I was crushing her. God led us to attend a church that was more open to women serving in the church, and even encouraged it. During this time my wife and I read the books 10 Lies the Church Tells Women by J. Lee Grady and Why Not Women? by Loren Cunningham, the founder of YWAM, whom I greatly respected.

Through these books, the Holy Spirit showed me the deeper truths that the Church has lost. Before the Fall, under God's original plan, men and women were created to have dominion together over the earth as equals (Gen. 1:26–28). It wasn't until after the Fall that women were subjugated to men as part of the curse (Gen. 3:16). Christ died to remove all curses (Gal. 3:13) in order to restore women to the original plan. Nevertheless, the Church has continued to embrace the curse mentality and has resisted accepting women in their rightful place of authority.

By understanding my wife's true position in Christ, I can champion her into her true destiny. We are now partners as we seek to expand the Kingdom of God here on earth.

Dan
AGE 48 CALIFORNIA, USA

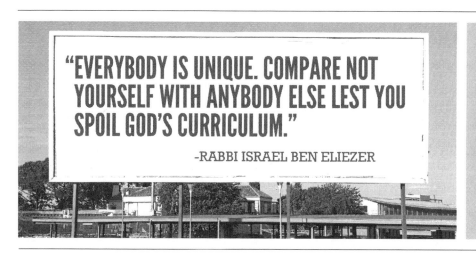

"EVERYBODY IS UNIQUE. COMPARE NOT YOURSELF WITH ANYBODY ELSE LEST YOU SPOIL GOD'S CURRICULUM."

-RABBI ISRAEL BEN ELIEZER

Men experience a felt need for respect, while women feel the need for love. In a survey of 7,000, 83% of men said they felt "disrespected" and 72% of women said they felt "unloved" in the midst of a conflict.

Source: http://loveandrespect.com/about-us/

INTERACT

What is one quality you love about being a man? How could this quality be designed to meet the needs of a woman in a relationship?

What is one masculine quality you think is most "misunderstood"?
How could this quality be designed to meet the needs of a woman in a relationship?

What is one quality (non-physical) you love about women? How could this quality be designed to meet the needs of a man in a relationship?

What is one feminine quality that you find frustrating or mystifying? How could this quality be designed to meet the needs of a man in a relationship?

MEN & WOMEN
TEST

	STRONGLY DISAGREE	MOSTLY DISAGREE	AGREE SOMEWHAT	MOSTLY AGREE	STRONGLY AGREE
I want to understand God's design for true masculinity and femininity.	1	2	3	4	5
I celebrate the fact that men and women are different.	1	2	3	4	5
I believe the differences between men and women are designed to work together in order to express the image of God.	1	2	3	4	5
My masculine qualities are designed to meet the needs of my future wife and our family.	1	2	3	4	5
My future wife's femininity is designed to meet my needs and the needs of our family .	1	2	3	4	5
When I encounter an aspect of masculinity or femininity that I don't understand, I don't put it down or ignore it; I look for its redemptive purpose.	1	2	3	4	5

Score:

(Note: Add up your scores after every ten days and evaluate your progress.)

ACTIVATION

There are some great resources out there to help you understand men's and women's needs better. Check out Shaunti Feldhahn's books For Men Only *and* For Women Only.

TALK TO GOD

Ask God to heal your heart from all attacks and misunderstandings around your identity as a man. Repent for any negative judgments you have made in your heart about men and women, and invite Him to lead you into a revelation of the beauty of masculinity and femininity.

"As people withhold their affection, a famine of love begins to grow in the land."
(page 149)

DAILY TRUTH
FEARLESS AFFECTION

Healthy touch and affection are basic human needs. And in a society where our technology continues to limit or remove normal human contact, where affection has been watered down and made extinct in most homes, and sadly, where unhealthy touch is all too common, meeting these needs can be difficult. However, there are healthy and safe ways of showing and receiving affection that you can and should cultivate.

It's important to realize that your need for healthy touch and affection is not the same as your need for sex. Sex is one way in which these needs can be met, but there are many other non-sexual forms of affection that you can and should be sharing on a regular basis with those close to you.

Healthy affection grows out of learning to see, honor, and serve others as fellow sons and daughters of the King. Seeing those around you in this way naturally encourages compassion, kindness, and encouragement. Treating guys like brothers and girls like sisters also helps to set good boundaries for healthy touch. The basic guideline for healthy touch is to show brotherly affection to guys and sisterly affection to girls. ★

SEE THOSE AROUND YOU AS ROYALTY...

Summary: Make it a point to show healthy affection to those you love on a daily basis.

SOUND WISDOM

...Be cheerful. Keep things in good repair. Keep your spirits up. Think in harmony. Be agreeable. Do all that, and the God of love and peace will be with you for sure. Greet one another with a holy embrace.

2 Corinthians 13:11–13

Jesus showed healthy touch and affection to those closest to Him, and received it as well. One of the most beautiful examples of this is seen at the Last Supper, which began with Jesus kneeling down and washing His disciples' feet. Later, while He and His guys all lay around the supper table talking and eating, one of them, John was actually lying right on Jesus' chest! Talk about touching and being touchable!

Jesus not only affirmed our need for affection; He demonstrated just how powerful and healing it can be. Jesus commissioned us, to continue His ministry of affection to a broken and hurting world. We need to follow His example and use our hands to bless, serve, heal, and comfort people. He wants His people to break the famine of healthy touch in the world and unleash an outpouring of His holy, healing affection!

REAL STORY

My first love language has always been touch. And growing up, I did just about whatever I could to get that need met. Sometimes it was totally healthy—i.e., hugs, pats on the back, tackling a friend. But when it came to girls, I couldn't enjoy a hug for what it was because I thought that enjoying it must mean I was attracted to that person. Nothing could be further from the truth! The last four years have brought me so much wisdom and revelation about this. Now I understand that needing to be touched is how I receive love. Touch has become an encouragement and a blessing for me.

When Katrina and I started dating we understood that touch was a way to give and receive love, but knew that our physical attraction could add some complications to this need. As much as I was physically attracted to this gorgeous woman, I also knew that in order to feel loved by her I didn't need to touch her all over. We were clear throughout our relationship that touch was a way to express our love, not our sexual desire.

While dating, we held hands and snuggled on the couch. I kissed her cheek and did what I could within our boundaries to affirm my love for her, and her for me. We did not kiss until we had both committed to marriage (after I proposed) and we withheld the ultimate prize of sex as a reward for our wedding night. In the end we both went to the marriage bed with a sense of purity, accomplishment, and trust in each other to love in every circumstance.

Doug
AGE 24 NORTH CAROLINA, USA

"AFFECTION IS RESPONSIBLE FOR NINE-TENTHS OF WHATEVER SOLID AND DURABLE HAPPINESS THERE IS IN OUR LIVES."

-C.S. LEWIS

Research by the University of Miami's Touch Research Institute has shown that human touch lessens pain, improves pulmonary function, increases growth in infants, lowers blood glucose and improves immune function.

Source: http://www.livestrong.com/

INTERACT

How affectionate was your home growing up?

Would you say you learned how to receive and give healthy affection?

What kind of affection is appropriate to show to a fellow son of the King?

What kind of affection is appropriate to show to a daughter of the King?

Where can you grow in showing affection?

TOUCH TEST

	STRONGLY DISAGREE	MOSTLY DISAGREE	AGREE SOMEWHAT	MOSTLY AGREE	STRONGLY AGREE
I am confident in showing non-sexual, friendly touch and affection to those around me.	1	2	3	4	5
I hug people often.	1	2	3	4	5
I want my hands to bless and comfort people, just as Christ's did.	1	2	3	4	5
The best way to counteract the lack of affection and the damage of inappropriate touch in our society is to show healthy, appropriate affection.	1	2	3	4	5
I am aware that I have a need for touch and affection.	1	2	3	4	5
I take responsibility and initiative in showing affection and getting my touch needs met in healthy ways.	1	2	3	4	5

Score:

(Note: Add up your scores after every ten days and evaluate your progress.)

ACTIVATION

Reach out and touch someone! Don't ignore opportunities to give and receive healthy affection with friends and loved ones today.

TALK TO GOD

Ask Jesus to lead you further into His ministry of healthy affection.

LAST SUNRISE OVER SEAS

June

I get discharged today and fly back to the States. Maria (the nurse) and I talked all night. We spent weeks together in the hospital building a friendship...we've grown really close. This morning she decided to watch the sunrise with me one last time. AMAZING! We always come to the same place on top of the highest peak, just minutes from town. You can see everything as the sun slowly rises in the distance. But this morning was different, Maria was oddly quiet, almost contemplative. Then, just as the sun rose over the rugged mountain peaks, Maria put my face in her hands, looked me right in the eyes, and said, "I DO!" It took me a few seconds to understand what she meant. Then it hit me like a ton of bricks...I started shouting "WOO HOOO!!! I think I woke up everyone in the hospital, but who cares... THIS IS THE BEST DAY OF MY LIFE!

"Learning to separate love and sex is the beginning of developing a healthy culture of holy affection." (page 154)

DAILY TRUTH
LOVE AND DESIRE

"Love" is a common excuse for out-of-bounds sex. Guys often say something like, "I love my girlfriend and she loves me. I can't imagine not being able to sleep with her." Or people say, "It's cruel to tell two people who love each other—man and woman, man and man, or woman and woman—that they can't have sex!" Most people who say such things also agree that sex and love is not the same thing, so the real issue is that they haven't yet learned to distinguish the difference between love and desire (passion).

Desire is a powerful thing, but love is more powerful still, because love is not a feeling or an urge; it is a choice. Love is the choice to think about and treat another person like God does, no matter the state of your desires and passions. What is more, love is a committed choice. Choices defined by your passions will change as your passions change, preventing you from making long-term commitments.

Test your heart as you work to govern your choices by love, not passion, in a relationship with a girl. As you think about her, ask, "Am I truly desiring God's best for her, whether that means having a relationship with her or not? Am I willing to make a commitment to love her no matter what? Or am I thinking about her in a selfish, conditional way, a way that is about her fulfilling my needs, desires, and fantasies?" ★

GOVERN YOUR CHOICES BY LOVE, NOT PASSION...

Summary: The more you train your desires to be loving, the more powerful and consistent you will be in cultivating deep, genuine, and holy friendships around you.

SOUND WISDOM

Many a man claims to have unfailing love, but a faithful man who can find? (Proverbs 20:6 NIV)

Wounds from a friend can be trusted, but an enemy multiplies kisses. (Proverbs 27:6 NIV)

Laugh with your happy friends when they're happy; share tears when they're down. Get along with each other; don't be stuck-up. Make friends with nobodies; don't be the great somebody. (Romans 12:15–16 MSG)

There are a lot of people in our society who mistake passion (emotional and sexual desire) for love, and then, when they don't feel passionate anymore, they abandon the relationship. Every great marriage is founded not only on passion, but upon friendship, and friendship is always founded upon trust, faithfulness, and commitment. If these factors are missing in your connection with your wife, you have a very broken relationship.

Friendships do not form overnight. You have to build some history with one another. You have to pass some tests and be proven trustworthy. The best friendships are the ones that have weathered the "best of times and the worst of times." If you want to have that kind of friendship with your wife, be sure to protect every stage of the relationship by demonstrating high levels of trustworthiness and commitment.

REAL STORY

When I look back on my life, I see that when I was in relationship with someone, I was focused on how much could I get, and how much they would give. After I took all I could out of them, I got bored with my partners, but I would stay with them out of guilt. I said I was staying because I loved them, but my love was conditional on how much they gave me sex, attention, or sacrifice, and how much they didn't inconvenience me. I would go out my way for them and fight for them, but only if I was getting what I wanted in return.

I was selfish.

After allowing God to reveal real love to me—real unconditional love—I have begun learning to stop putting myself first. My priority in a relationship is not to get something from someone, but to encourage, support and bless my partner. I want to help her fulfill her dreams, knowing that she will do the same for me.

I have learned that love means "not doing" as much as it does "doing." As I manage my sex drive and refuse to sexualize women, I am training myself to love the woman of my dreams and focus all my love toward her. Sex is not love. Sex outside of love says "satisfy me," whereas sex in marriage is an expression of love that says, "Let me satisfy you and your needs."

Parker
AGE 25 CALIFORNIA, USA

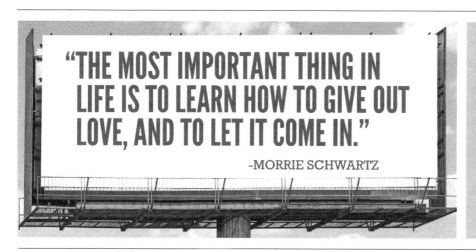

"THE MOST IMPORTANT THING IN LIFE IS TO LEARN HOW TO GIVE OUT LOVE, AND TO LET IT COME IN."

-MORRIE SCHWARTZ

In a 2004 Zogby poll, 91% of parents said teens should be taught that the best choice is for sexual activity to be linked to love, intimacy, and commitment—qualities most likely to occur in faithful marriage.
Source: Bridget Maher.

INTERACT

How does the test of commitment expose whether you are acting out of love or passion?

Do you have a best friend (friends)? Describe a time in your friendship in which you have shared the following:

1) "Wounds from a friend…":

2) "Laugh with your happy friends…":

3) "[Sharing] tears…":

LOVE & DESIRE
TEST

	STRONGLY DISAGREE	MOSTLY DISAGREE	AGREE SOMEWHAT	MOSTLY AGREE	STRONGLY AGREE
My desires may feel loving, but they are only really loving if they align with God's best.	1	2	3	4	5
It's my responsibility to train my desires to align with God's best.	1	2	3	4	5
I am careful not to confuse love with desire, sexual or otherwise.	1	2	3	4	5
Being a real lover to a woman requires me to be capable of holding up my end of a loyal friendship.	1	2	3	4	5
I want my loyalty to Christ to stand the test of time, conflict, and sacrifice.	1	2	3	4	5
I have a best friend(s) who is much more than a buddy; our friendship has stood the test of time, conflict, and sacrifice.	1	2	3	4	5

Score:

(Note: Add up your scores after every ten days and evaluate your progress.)

ACTIVATION

Do something thoughtful for your best friend today.

TALK TO GOD

Ask God to deepen your understanding of and desire for His best in your closest relationships.

"...there is no such thing as an unwanted child."
(page 182)

DAILY TRUTH
CONTENDING FOR YOUR CHILDREN

You are living in a generation that is fundamentally at war over the family, and even more basically, over the value of human life. In this war, you have three options: 1) You can become one of the war's many victims, most of whom are brainwashed into becoming perpetrators. 2) You can build your own little castle against the world and do everything you can to protect your family and loved ones from the war. Or, 3) You can become a hero who signs up for battle and receives his Commander's orders as to where He knows you can advance the victory.

The war must be won in your own heart before you can bring victory to others, and that war is over your choice to value, love, and protect human life, and then marriage and family, as God does. Do you really understand and believe that every human person— great or small, young or old, smart or slow, powerful or weak—has the highest value in all creation in God's eyes? He forever defined and established our value to Him when He gave up His Son—the most valuable thing in the universe—for us. Our lives either have the greatest value of all, or they have no value. You must choose one or the other, and then you must work that value into your every thought and action. ★

HE KNOWS YOU CAN ADVANCE THE VICTORY...

Summary: Establishing God's value for human life will position you to protect and honor it. You are called to restore His value to the hearts of a devalued generation.

SOUND WISDOM

The people brought children to Jesus, hoping he might touch them. The disciples shooed them off. But Jesus was irate and let them know it: "Don't push these children away. Don't ever get between them and me. These children are at the very center of life in the kingdom. Mark this: Unless you accept God's kingdom in the simplicity of a child, you'll never get in."

Mark 10:13–16 MSG

If you love Jesus, you will love kids, because Jesus loves kids. In fact, all through the Bible God emphasizes His heart of jealous protection for children, particularly the orphaned and fatherless. He has some pretty frightening things to say to those who exploit and abandon children too. Suffice to say, God's maternal and paternal "instinct" is quite intact, and you don't want to mess with His kids!

Invite God to reveal His protective love for His children to you. Invite Jesus to restore the heart of a child within you so that you can value children as He does. And then ask your Father how you can work with Him to protect and care for the orphaned and fatherless, and introduce them to their true home in the Father's house. May you be one who helps to restore God's value for children in your generation.

REAL STORY

There was a time that I had little value for life, especially the life of a baby or a child. I thought abortion was no big deal and I didn't care if I ever became a father. The thought of me being a father and having someone's life in my hands scared me. Then God spoke to me and said, "You don't like who you are. You don't think you have anything to offer a child." I didn't have to think about this long, because I knew it was true. I never liked who I thought I was, and I struggled with drugs, alcohol and sex-addictive behaviors in my not-so-distant past. My identity was based on my sin, not on who God said I am. So I went after truth.

I started embracing the role of spiritual father, though I still wasn't sure I had what it took to become a father of my own child…until I had an amazing encounter during worship one night. I was laid out on the pulpit and all the children in the church came up and sat around me even sat on my lap. In that moment God spoke to me and said, "You are ready to be a father, not just a spiritual father." I immediately received my role as a father into my heart. Less than two weeks later, my wife got pregnant. As I watched my little baby grow inside her, my father heart started to explode. I started to understand for the first time the value of life and how I was made to protect it. Now that I've watched my little girl grow inside my wife, abortion takes on a whole new meaning. It was very clear to me that life began the day of conception and that's the day I became a father.

Jason
AGE 37 INDIANA, USA

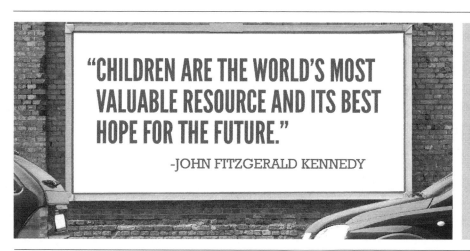

"CHILDREN ARE THE WORLD'S MOST VALUABLE RESOURCE AND ITS BEST HOPE FOR THE FUTURE."

-JOHN FITZGERALD KENNEDY

Nearly half of pregnancies among American women are unintended, and about four in 10 of these are terminated by abortion. Twenty-two percent of all pregnancies (excluding miscarriages) end in abortion.

Source: http://www.guttmacher.org

INTERACT

Give three examples of how you have seen human life treated as having little value in the world around you:

1)

2)

3)

What are three benefits that having children brings into your life?

1)

2)

3)

What are some characteristics of the child's heart Jesus told us to have?

CHILDREN TEST

	STRONGLY DISAGREE	MOSTLY DISAGREE	AGREE SOMEWHAT	MOSTLY AGREE	STRONGLY AGREE
Human life is a gift from God, and has the highest value.	1	2	3	4	5
All children are a blessing from God.	1	2	3	4	5
I want to do my part to honor, protect, and fight for the value of human life, particularly those who are weak and vulnerable.	1	2	3	4	5
I want to do my part to restore the value for children in our society.	1	2	3	4	5
Parenthood is a high calling from God and I will do my utmost to love and raise the children God gives me, whether spiritual, natural, or adopted.	1	2	3	4	5
I am pursuing a childlike heart.	1	2	3	4	5

Score:

(Note: Add up your scores after every ten days and evaluate your progress.)

ACTIVATION

There are a million fronts where you can get behind the fight for the value of human life and the value for children, but the best place to start is where you are. If you don't love the children around you, you're probably not going to dive right into rescuing sex slaves or orphans. Begin looking for where your life is already touching children or issues of injustice, and ask what you can do to help.

TALK TO GOD

Ask the Lord where He wants you to serve in the battle over the value of human life and the value of children.

"…they developed a purity plan for themselves, and they asked…if we would hold them accountable for the plan. We told them we would, but only under the condition that they would work harder to keep their virginity than we would." (page 192)

DAILY TRUTH
ACCOUNTABILITY AS A COUPLE

When your relationship with a girl becomes serious, it's a good idea to look for a person or couple who can help you on a consistent basis as you chart the course for your relationship. They could be your parents, your pastors, counselors, or just a couple in your community, but they should have a loving, healthy marriage, and be people you both admire and trust. In particular, they should share your value for purity and marriage and be able to encourage you that your commitment to wait for God's best is absolutely worth the wait! These voices of encouragement will add incredible strength to you both as you manage your desires.

As with all healthy relationships, this older couple or person should never be responsible to control or police you both as you protect your purity. It is your responsibility to pursue and invite open communication about how you're managing your desires.

Not only can these experienced friends offer the benefits of their "lessons learned"; they can help to remind you that marriage is not only about leaving your families to start a new family, but also about becoming a new unit within a rich tapestry of relationships.

Marriages thrive when you as individuals and as a couple are connected to other healthy individuals and couples outside the marriage. ★

GOD'S BEST IS ABSOLUTELY WORTH THE WAIT…

Summary: Pursue relationships with couples who have the kind of relationship you hope to have with one another.

SOUND WISDOM

Take good counsel and accept correction— that's the way to live wisely and well. (Proverbs 19:20 MSG)

Form your purpose by asking for counsel, then carry it out using all the help you can get. (Proverbs 20:18 MSG)

It's better to be wise than strong; intelligence outranks muscle any day. Strategic planning is the key to warfare; to win, you need a lot of good counsel. (Proverbs 24:5–6 MSG)

It is important to develop a purity plan that you both agree upon as a couple, a plan that accounts for your individual needs and limits. Be as honest as you can about what you need! If there's a situation that you are even 50% sure will push your sex drive into overdrive, then admit it and agree to save those moments for after your "I dos."

After you draw up your joint plan, invite your trusted, older and wiser friends to sit down with you and go over the plan. Then decide on how often you will check in with each other to see how things are going and adjust your plan as needed. When you create a strong team around you in this way, you and your lady will be unstoppable in carrying your purity trophy from the battlefield to the bedroom!

REAL STORY

Before my wife I had a couple serious relationships. I always knew I would not give away my virginity to anyone except my wife, so that part of purity was never in question for me. But unfortunately there was other stuff I did, because I didn't really have a plan. I thought, "Well, I just won't have sex," but just having that boundary ended up not being enough. With those relationships I did things physically and emotionally that I'm not proud of, and gave a part of myself away that I will never get back.

So by the time I met my wife, I had learned that no matter how "strong" I thought I was, I still needed to have a plan for how I was going to be responsible with myself. Early in our relationship we made some clear boundaries to protect each other. The most important boundary was that we would not kiss on the lips until we got married. Making this decision was not just out of our pure will. We prayed and both felt the Lord give us the grace to do it. It allowed our emotional relationship to build and become strong without the physical part becoming a distraction. I found myself falling more and more in love with my wife every day. I truly found myself in love with who she was and not just excited about the newness of a relationship. There were times when I really wanted to kiss her, but I knew that it would be so worth the wait. I'm so thankful we did, because on our wedding day when we kissed for the first time, I felt like I won the best prize ever: my wife.

Sal
AGE 29 CALIFORNIA, USA

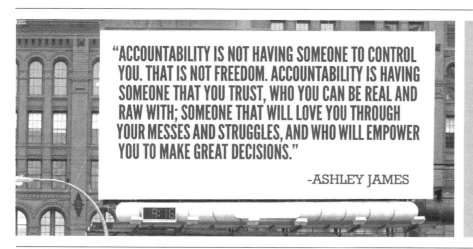

"ACCOUNTABILITY IS NOT HAVING SOMEONE TO CONTROL YOU. THAT IS NOT FREEDOM. ACCOUNTABILITY IS HAVING SOMEONE THAT YOU TRUST, WHO YOU CAN BE REAL AND RAW WITH; SOMEONE THAT WILL LOVE YOU THROUGH YOUR MESSES AND STRUGGLES, AND WHO WILL EMPOWER YOU TO MAKE GREAT DECISIONS."

–ASHLEY JAMES

Mentor Couples can help couples avoid a bad marriage before it begins and pre-pare for a life-long marriage, strengthen existing marriages, restore 80% to 90% of the worst marriages, help 70% of the separated to reconcile, and enable four out of five step-families to be successful.

Source: http://www.marriagesavers.org

INTERACT

Name the people in your life who are rooting for you in your battle for purity.

How does their hope and faith in you affect your motivation and decisions as you manage your desires?

Name one couple whose marriage you admire. Describe a few specific things about their relationship that you hope to share in your marriage.

Do you struggle with either the idea of making a purity plan with your girlfriend or inviting input on the plan from trusted friends? If so, can you identify why?

COUPLE
TEST

	STRONGLY DISAGREE	MOSTLY DISAGREE	AGREE SOMEWHAT	MOSTLY AGREE	STRONGLY AGREE
Marriage is a relationship that is deeply connected to other relationships, so it's important to honor these connections as I move toward marriage.	1	2	3	4	5
I have people in my life who are rooting for me to be successful in honoring purity and who help to remind me that the battle is worth it.	1	2	3	4	5
It is irresponsible not to have a plan for purity as a couple. We need to know each other's limits and how to honor them.	1	2	3	4	5
I will do whatever I need to do to protect my purity and the purity of my future wife.	1	2	3	4	5
I look for successful marriages to emulate.	1	2	3	4	5
It's important for me to be able to live out loud with those I love and trust and share both my struggles and my victories with them.	1	2	3	4	5

Score:
(Note: Add up your scores after every ten days and evaluate your progress.)

ACTIVATION

If you are in a relationship and you either don't have a purity plan or don't have a couple you are sharing your courtship journey with, then pick one of these things to start working on. If you're not in a relationship, start making note of possible couples whose input you would like to have in making your purity plan when the time comes.

TALK TO GOD

Ask Him to lead you to the perfect people who will encourage you, remind you that you can have an amazing marriage, and help you move toward it.

"You can never fall so far that you can't be restored. Whether you have lived a life like Grace's or you have just failed your own standards, you need to understand how to clean up your mess and get yourself back on the Holy Highway again." (page 194)

DAILY TRUTH
RESTORING THE STANDARD

The story of the Prodigal Son is probably the most famous restoration story in the Bible. Here it is:

There was once a man who had two sons. The younger said to his father, "Father, I want right now what's coming to me." So the father divided the property between them. It wasn't long before the younger son packed his bags and left for a distant country. There, undisciplined and dissipated, he wasted everything he had.

After he had gone through all his money, there was a bad famine all through that country and he began to hurt. He signed on with a citizen there who assigned him to his fields to slop the pigs. He was so hungry he would have eaten the corncobs in the pig slop, but no one would give him any. That brought him to his senses. He said, 'All those farmhands working for my father sit down to three meals a day, and here I am starving to death. I'm going back to my father. I'll say to him, Father, I've sinned against God, I've sinned before you; I don't deserve to be called your son. Take me on as a hired hand.'

He got right up and went home to his father. When he was still a long way off, his father saw him. His heart pounding, he ran out, embraced him, and kissed him. The son started his speech: "Father, I've sinned against God, I've sinned before you; I don't deserve to be called your son ever again."

But the father wasn't listening. He was calling to the servants, "Quick. Bring a clean set of clothes and dress him. Put the family ring on his finger and sandals on his feet. Then get a grain-fed heifer and roast it. We're going to feast! We're going to have a wonderful time! My son is here—given up for dead and now alive! Given up for lost and now found!" And they began to have a wonderful time. (Luke 15:11–24 MSG)

This story is a picture of how God restores His sons and daughters. He doesn't just restore them to the position of servants. He doesn't give them a second-class place in the home. He restores them to their full rank and privileges as His children.

GOD RESTORES HIS SONS & DAUGHTERS...

He removes their rags of shame and clothes them in righteousness and purity. He restores their ring of identity and authority. He gives them shoes of protection and health. And then He draws them into a life of celebration and joy that heals their hearts of all their painful memories and makes room for them to begin a new life as wise, holy children. ★

Summary: God's ability to restore and renew is so much greater than our perception of what we think we deserve.

REAL STORY

About three and a half years ago, a sequence of events began that would ultimately change my life forever. At that time, I was living with my girlfriend who, in all honesty, I hooked up with in a one night stand. We both grew up in church and knew that how we were living was wrong, but we wanted it to work so we made up every excuse we could to make it seem okay. Fast-forward to right now. We are still together, we are madly in love with each other, and even greater, we are insanely in love with God. We have huge hearts to help others transform their relationships to allow God to be at the center. How did all of this happen? God. Only God could pour out enough grace in our relationship to completely transform it to one of purity, honor, and covenant.

We allowed God to basically put our relationship in reverse and then slowly rebuild it, all the while changing our beliefs and mindsets. This isn't an easy process, especially when couples stay together like Libby and I did. We moved out and became physically pure with each other, which meant no sex, no foreplay, and during certain time periods, no kissing and no hand-holding. During this time God taught me that I needed to know myself before I could attempt to understand someone else. I had Libby in my "God spot." I looked to her for everything— joy, happiness, value, confirmation, and even guidance. I had to come to the understanding that only God can be in the God spot. I had to learn what it meant to have an identity as a son of God. According to everyone we knew, our relationship should have ended. According to any statistic you can find, our relationship shouldn't have worked out. But the great news is God is a God who works with the impossible and makes it possible. Only through God could this relationship work out the way it did. Because of Jesus I was given enough grace to cover my sinful past and pursue a future relationship with purity, honor, and a covenant.

John
AGE 23 FLORIDA, USA

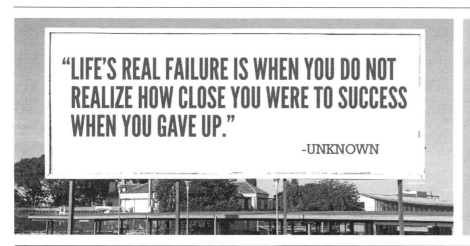

"LIFE'S REAL FAILURE IS WHEN YOU DO NOT REALIZE HOW CLOSE YOU WERE TO SUCCESS WHEN YOU GAVE UP."

–UNKNOWN

Forgiveness has been associated with lower heart rate and blood pressure, greater relief from stress, decrease in medication use, improved sleep quality and decrease in fatigue, and reduction in depressive symptoms.

Source: http://purposebeyondpain.com

INTERACT

In order to experience your Father's restoration, you need to take the following steps:

1. Confess and renounce every lie that disqualifies you from full restoration to your position and inheritance as a son of the King. "I've made too many mistakes. I'm too damaged. I don't deserve a happy life, marriage, family, etc." Jesus vigorously disagrees on every point. He put people in the Bible like Moses, David, and Paul—former murderers and adulterers—to show you what he can do with people who have done a lot worse stuff than you.

2. Confess and renounce your sin. Sin involves attaching your desires to the wrong object. Many people find it difficult to surrender the thing that has brought them a measure of pleasure or comfort because they can't conceive or trust that God has something so much better for them. But He does—He has the fulfillment your desires were designed for in the first place.

3. Receive and extend forgiveness. Jesus made it clear that receiving and giving forgiveness go together. We have all sinned and been sinned against, and we must extend the grace of Christ to ourselves and to others alike.

4. Surrender your life to your Father. Invite Him to carry out His restoration process in your life. Commit to letting Him raise you to think and act like a son. Commit to receiving His love and looking to Him as your first source of comfort and affection. Commit to letting Him show you the way of love in every area, including the area of managing your sex drive and your desire for marriage and family.

5. Fight the fight of faith every day. Do you think the Prodigal Son immediately felt at home in his father's house after being restored? It's unlikely. It takes a while to accept that you deserve the status, righteousness, and blessing the Father has given you. It takes a while to realize that your failures and wounds simply cannot keep you from being who He made and restored you to be. You have to keep submitting your feelings and memories to the foot of the cross and to the word of God over your life. You deserve everything He has given you, simply because He says so and made it possible!

RESTORATION TEST

	STRONGLY DISAGREE	MOSTLY DISAGREE	AGREE SOMEWHAT	MOSTLY AGREE	STRONGLY AGREE
When God looks at me, He doesn't see my mistakes. He sees Jesus.	1	2	3	4	5
God doesn't want me to be ashamed of my mistakes; He wants me to learn from them.	1	2	3	4	5
Sexual sin cannot disqualify me from experiencing God's best for my sex life, if I receive His restoration.	1	2	3	4	5
I can speak about my mistakes without shame.	1	2	3	4	5
I want to be willing to give up anything, no matter how good, in order to receive God's best for me.	1	2	3	4	5
Forgiving myself and others for sin is very important to me. I do my best to make sure that I am not carrying shame, bitterness, or judgment in my heart toward myself or anyone else.	1	2	3	4	5

Score:

(Note: Add up your scores after every ten days and evaluate your progress.)

INTERACT & TALK TO GOD

Invite the Holy Spirit to lead you through the steps of restoration listed above. Ask Him first if you have believed any lies that would disqualify you from experiencing the fullness of life in the Father's house as a restored son of God:

Now invite the Holy Spirit to help you confess and renounce any past sins you have committed. Ask Him to help you identify the roots of these behaviors, and to give you wisdom and revelation to uproot them and replace them with His truth and love. You can write your confession below if you like, or any insights you hear from the Holy Spirit:

Ask the Holy Spirit if there is anyone you need to forgive for any reason, including yourself. Break off all judgments you have made toward them, forgive them, and bless them in Jesus' name. Invite Jesus to pour out His grace in that relationship.

Make the following declarations:

1. I recognize that in living a righteous life, dying, and rising from the dead, Jesus paid the full penalty for my sin and restored me as a son of God.

2. I recognize that my old, dead nature was crucified with Him on the cross and that now, by faith, I share in His life, His nature, His righteousness, and His status before the Father.

3. I recognize that there is absolutely nothing that can separate me from the love of my Father and that I deserve everything He gives me because of what Christ did for me.

4. My Father has given me all that is His—His Spirit, His nature, His love, His kingdom. He has provided for my body, soul, and spirit to be 100% whole and filled with abundant life.

5. My Father is committed not only to restoring me of every harmful effect of sin in my life, but of teaching me to be wise and victorious over every deceiving lie that would lead me into sin.

6. I declare that I deserve God's absolute best for me in my sexuality and that no past mistakes can keep me from experiencing the fullness of His design for my body, my marriage, and my family.

7. I declare that I will trust God's word over my life above every other voice, feeling, or circumstance and allow Him to define my identity and my destiny.

8. I declare that as I trust in Christ's strength and receive His grace to live like He lives, I will honor God's design for sex and marriage in my thoughts, words, and actions.

DAY 40
★

"A covenant is an agreement made between two parties where both parties have the right and the responsibility to carry out certain commitments to fulfill a desired outcome." (page 90)

DAILY TRUTH
MAKING A COVENANT

Marriage is a covenant. Besides your covenant relationship with God, marriage is the most important covenant you will make in your life. Making and walking out a covenant obviously requires you to be a person who keeps promises, a person who does what he says he will do. It requires you to commit—not just at the altar, but every day that follows. The wonderful thing is that the very act of committing creates the opportunity for the best in you to rise up and help you walk it out. Many people in our society are afraid of commitment because they fear they don't have what it takes to keep their promises. But you, as a son of the faithful, covenant-making God, can be absolutely sure that you have what it takes to commit, to promise.

However, becoming a faithful man of your word doesn't happen overnight. By the time you stand at the altar, you want to know that both you and the woman you're gazing at have a proven track record of doing what you say you're going to do. This is why it is so important that you start today to prepare for

the covenant of marriage, as you also learn to walk in covenant with God.

The commitments you're invited to make with God today about your purity are designed to work in the context of your eternal covenant with the Father through Christ. This isn't a simple "virginity pledge" where you're making a promise to yourself to be pure. This is a two-way commitment between you and God, and the best part is that you can be absolutely certain that He will uphold His end of the agreement! Not only that, He will give you the grace to uphold yours.

Summary: When God wanted to guarantee his promises to you, he gave his word—a rock-solid guarantee, because God can't break his word. (Heb. 6:16–18 MSG)

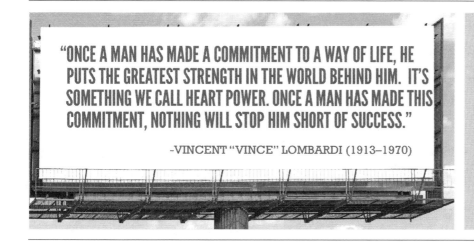

"ONCE A MAN HAS MADE A COMMITMENT TO A WAY OF LIFE, HE PUTS THE GREATEST STRENGTH IN THE WORLD BEHIND HIM. IT'S SOMETHING WE CALL HEART POWER. ONCE A MAN HAS MADE THIS COMMITMENT, NOTHING WILL STOP HIM SHORT OF SUCCESS."

-VINCENT "VINCE" LOMBARDI (1913–1970)

A true commitment means being willing to make sacrifices and do what it takes to make a relationship work. Committed couples are significantly more likely to have lasting and happy marriages.`

Source: http://psychcentral.com

AGREEMENTS:

- Father, I agree that you designed and created my whole being—spirit, soul, and body—including my sexuality, and that You said it was very good. I am powerful, valuable, worthy of Your love, and worthy of an amazing marriage.

- I agree that Your guidelines for my sexuality will lead me to Your best for my life.

- I agree that You designed sex, not only as the means of procreation, but as an act of love that establishes a complete spirit, soul, and body bond between a man and a woman. For this reason, sex ought to be expressed solely within the boundaries of a life-long marriage covenant.

PLEDGES:

- I pledge to trust You, my Father, as the One who fulfills my desires. I will look to You as my ultimate source of affection, comfort, happiness, peace, identity, and hope.

- I pledge to honor Your design for my sexuality in word, thought, and action. I will steward my physical, emotional, and spiritual desires according to Your guidelines so that they consistently propel me toward a godly marriage.

- I pledge to honor others as fellow sons and daughters of the King, treating them as I wish to be treated, no matter how they treat me. I will think of them with pure thoughts and look at them with pure eyes, as You do. I will not compromise Your standards for my sexuality for anyone, even myself.

- I pledge to carry myself as a royal son whose body, soul, and spirit belong first to You, then to me, and then to the woman I marry. I will not give myself sexually, even in my mind and heart, to any woman but my wife.

RECOGNITION:

- I recognize that You have made every provision for me to manage my sex drive well and become fully prepared to experience sex and marriage as You designed them. I can do all things through Christ's strength (see Phil. 4:13).

- I recognize that You have promised to fulfill the desires of my heart as I delight in You (see Ps. 37:4), including my desires for sex and marriage.

- I recognize that You have promised to provide a way of escape from every temptation (see 1 Cor. 10:13).

- I recognize that You have promised to fully forgive and restore me after every failure. You invite me to come before You boldly when I need Your mercy and grace (see Heb. 4:16).

- I recognize that You are always with me, that nothing can separate me from Your love, that I hear Your voice, that I am fully accepted by You no matter what I do, and that You always delight in me.

TALK TO GOD

After reading through the statements above, invite the Holy Spirit to seal the covenant you have made with Him and respond to your words. Receive His delight in you and His strength to make you successful in honoring what you have said.

COVENANT
TEST

	STRONGLY DISAGREE	MOSTLY DISAGREE	AGREE SOMEWHAT	MOSTLY AGREE	STRONGLY AGREE
Being a man of my word is very important to me.	1	2	3	4	5
I am not afraid of making promises, because I know that God will give me the grace to keep them.	1	2	3	4	5
Honoring my wife now, before we are married or even before I know who she is, will set me up for a successful marriage.	1	2	3	4	5
Committing to things brings out the best in me.	1	2	3	4	5
I know God will not only uphold His end of our covenant; He will give me what I need to uphold my end. Even when I grow weak, I know He is strong.	1	2	3	4	5
Even though I live in a society of broken covenants, I can be a man who honors and upholds my covenants with God and others.	1	2	3	4	5

Score:

(Note: Add up your scores after every ten days and evaluate your progress.)

ACTIVATION

Choose a meaningful, tangible symbol of your purity covenant, such as a promise ring, that you can wear or otherwise see on a daily basis.

EVALUATION

DAY 31	
DAY 32	
DAY 33	
DAY 34	
DAY 35	
DAY 36	
DAY 37	
DAY 38	
DAY 39	
DAY 40	
TOTAL: (300 Possible)	

Congratulations! You have made it through the whole journal! Now's your chance to go back and add up your scores from your last 10 self-evaluation tests.

How have the last forty days changed your thinking or behavior?

OUR BIG DAY!!!

August

Like a kid waiting for Christmas, here I sit in this surreal moment of anticipation, eagerly waiting for "the day" to come. I've literally waited my whole life, worked four hard years and fought through the darkness of war, all in pursuit of love. It's easy to look back and not only see how far I've come, but why I've stayed my course. Seeing visions of Maria emerging from the diamond and the hope that somehow she was real fueled an unquenchable fire in me. It was as if nothing else mattered except laying down my life for someone I didn't even know, and now she's here... Tomorrow she has no idea that I'm about to give her my entire life in one symbol, the ring!

ABOUT MORAL

THE FACTS

1 Cars & Contraception (60's)

In the 1950's, access to cars gave teenagers an independence unknown to the previous generation. When "the pill" came on the scene in 1960, women stopped requiring men to marry them before having sex because they no longer feared getting pregnant.

3 First US State Legalizes "No-Fault" Divorce (1970)

In 1970, Governor Ronald Reagan passed the "no-fault" divorce law in the state of California allowing marriages to be dissolved without providing proof that a breach in the marital contract had occurred. By 1985, all other states would follow. Currently, the US has an overall divorce rate of 50%. The US ranks 6th in the world for highest divorce rates.

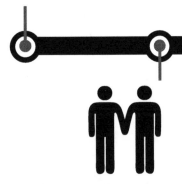

2 First US State Legalizes Sodomy (Homosexual Acts) (1962)

In 1962, Illinois became the first state to remove criminal penalties for consensual sodomy (homosexual acts) from their criminal code. Today, about 3.8% of Americans identify as gay, lesbian, bisexual, or transgender.

4 Supreme Court Legalizes Abortion (1973)

In 1973 abortion became legal in our nation. Since the 40th anniversary of Roe vs. Wade, the US has aborted over 54 million children. In 1995, Norma McCorvey (Roe) became a Christian. She is now pro-life. In 2005, she petitioned the Supreme Court to overturn Roe vs. Wade... her petition was denied.

REVOLUTION

5 STD's and Children Born Out of Wedlock (70's – Present)

Prior to the Sexual Revolution, there were two main STDs that people were concerned about contracting. Now, there are over 25. That's more than a 1,200% increase in 50 years. Today, 1 in 4 people are infected with an STD. In 1964, only 7% of children were born out of wedlock... today, 53% of children are born in the U.S. out of wedlock.

7 Sex Slavery (Today)

There are currently over 27 million people, in 161 countries, trapped in the sex slave industry around the globe. People are sold as slaves for $90 or less. 80% of these slaves are women. 17,500 people are trafficked into the US annually. Sex slavery is a 32 billion dollar industry worldwide.

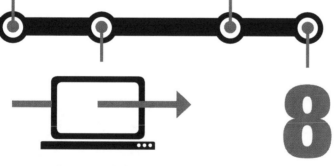

6 Internet/Porn Industry (1995 – Present)

With the launch of the internet and with the increasing popularity of smartphones, porn has now become a 5 billion dollar world-wide industry. 7 out of 10 men and 5 out of 10 women view porn regularly. Sex is the #1 topic searched on the internet.

8 THE NEW SEX RADICAL

A PERSON RADICAL ENOUGH TO QUESTION EVERYTHING AROUND THEM & GET BACK TO GOD'S ORIGINAL INTENT & DESIGN FOR GENDER, SEXUALITY, MARRIAGE, & THE FAMILY.

FOUNDER'S NOTE

Moral Revolution is an organization of radical lovers and passionate people. Like Dr. Martin Luther King, we have a dream of becoming a catalyst for a liberating global movement. We are committed to transforming how the world views sexuality, defines the unborn, embraces the family, and values all generations by honoring every human life.

We have dedicated ourselves to uncovering the root causes of moral decay that destroy the very fabric of our society. We have united under the banner of true love to help provide real solutions to these core issues and not just symptomatic cures.

It is our heart-felt conviction that a healthy culture is nurtured by positive reinforcement through intelligent and unbiased education. Honest, transparent discussion will achieve far more than fear, punishment, and rules.

WE BELIEVE THAT WHEN MOST PEOPLE ARE LOVED UNCONDITIONALLY, EQUIPPED PROPERLY, INFORMED EQUITABLY, AND EMPOWERED EQUALLY, THEY ARE PRONE TO BEHAVE NOBLY.

JOIN THE REVOLUTION, AND TOGETHER WE WILL MAKE HISTORY!

CHANGING GLOBAL MINDSETS BY CHANGING CULTURE

FAMILY

CHURCH

CULTURE

EDUCATION

GOVERNMENT

START

LITTLE ME

LEARN IT

LOVE IT

WEBSITE PODCAST CONFERENCES

LIVE IT

40-DAY JOURNAL

LEAD IT

REVOLUTIONIST

LEADERSHIP CURRICULUM LEADERSHIP WORKSHOPS

STAY CONNECTED

website

facebook

twitter @MORALREVOLUTION

youtube

podcast

blog

email CONTACT@MORALREVOLUTION.COM

ADDITIONAL RESOURCES

MORAL REVOLUTION

This book takes a non-religious, gut-honest, fresh look at a subject as old as Adam and Eve. The wisdom within helps you and those you love emerge from the mire with your trophy of purity intact so you can present it to your lover on your honeymoon. While some nations seem to live in a perpetual orgy, and religion relegates the masses to sexual prison, people need to know they can overcome the power of peer pressure and push back the cesspool of distorted cultural values. You can take a Vow of Purity today—you will never regret the decision.

MORAL REVOLUTION COURSES

Moral Revolution Courses is a brand new series of resources designed to equip and train Youth Pastors, Leaders, Parents, and Educators. You will learn how to better teach and influence those you lead on many tough subjects, often abandoned by the church. Sexuality is the first course and covers six sessions.

NOW AVAILABLE

REQUEST A SPEAKER

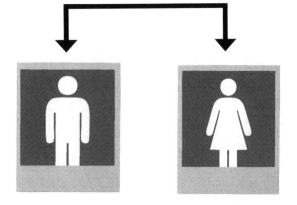

ADD AN ELEMENT

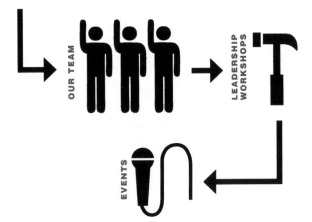

For more info, email: contact@moralrevolution.com

Join the MORAL REVOLUTION AND TOGETHER WE WILL MAKE HISTORY

NEWSLETTER PRAY  DONATE

Made in the USA
San Bernardino, CA
21 April 2016